CANTERBURY STUDIES IN ANGLICANISM

Christ and Culture

CANTERBURY STUDIES
IN ANGLICANISM

Series Editors:
Martyn Percy and Ian Markham

Christ and Culture

Edited by
Martyn Percy, Mark Chapman,
Ian Markham and Barney Hawkins

Morehouse Publishing

CANTERBURY
PRESS
Norwich

First published in 2010 by the Canterbury Press Norwich
Editorial office
13–17 Long Lane, London, EC1A 9PN, UK
Canterbury Press is an imprint of Hymns Ancient and Modern Ltd
(a registered charity)
St Mary's Works, St Mary's Plain, Norwich, NR3 3BH, UK
www.scm-canterburypress.co.uk

First published in North America in 2010 by
Morehouse Publishing, 4775 Linglestown Road,
Harrisburg, PA 17112
Morehouse Publishing, 445 Fifth Avenue, New York, NY 10016
Morehouse Publishing is an imprint of
Church Publishing Incorporated.
www.morehousepublishing.org

Library of Congress Cataloging-in-Publication Data

A catalog record for this book is available
from the Library of Congress.

Morehouse ISBN: 978-0-8192-2397-5
Canterbury ISBN: 978-1-85311-948-4

Typeset by Manila Typesetting Company
Printed in the United States of America

10 11 12 13 14 15   10 9 8 7 6 5 4 3 2 1

CONTENTS

FOREWORD TO THE SERIES
by the Archbishop of Canterbury

The question, 'What is the real identity of Anglicanism?' has become more pressing and more complex than ever before in the last decade or so, ecumenically as well as internally. Is the Anglican identity a matter of firm Reformed or Calvinist principle, resting its authoritative appeal on a conviction about the sovereignty and all-sufficiency of Scripture interpreted literally? Is it a form of non-papal Catholicism, strongly focused on sacramental and ministerial continuity, valuing the heritage not only of primitive Christianity but also of mediaeval and even post-Reformation Catholic practice and devotion? Is it an essentially indeterminate Christian culture, particularly well-adapted to the diversity of national and local sympathies and habits? Is the whole idea of an 'ism' misplaced here?

Each of these models has its defenders across the Communion; and each has some pretty immediate consequences for the polity and politics of the global Anglican family. Some long for a much more elaborately confessional model than has generally been the case – the sort of model that those who defined the boundaries of the Church of England in the sixteenth century were very wary of. Some are happy with the idea of the Communion becoming a federation of local bodies with perhaps, in the long run, quite markedly diverging theologies and disciplines. The disagreements over the ordination of women and the Church's response to lesbian and gay people have raised basic issues around the liberty of local churches to decide what are thought by many to be secondary matters; the problem then being that not everyone

agrees that they are secondary. The question of identity is inseparable from the question of unity: to recognize another community as essentially the same, whatever divergences there may be
in language and practice, is necessary for any unity that is more
than formal – for a unity that issues in vigorous evangelism and
consistent 'diaconal' service to the world.

And this means in turn that questions about Anglican identity
will inevitably become questions about the very nature of the
Church – and thus the nature of revelation and incarnation and
the character of God's activity. I believe it is generally a piece of
deplorably overheated rhetoric to describe those holding different views around the kind of questions I have mentioned as being
adherents of 'different religions'; but there is an uncomfortable
sense in which this exaggeration reminds us that the line between
primary and secondary issues is not self-evidently clear – or at
least that what we say about apparently secondary matters may
reveal something about our primary commitments.

The long and short of it is that we should be cautious of saying
of this or that development or practice 'It isn't Anglican', as if
that settled the matter. One of the first tasks we need to pursue
in the current climate is simply to look at what Anglicans say
and do. We need to watch Anglicans worshipping, constructing
patterns for decision-making and administration, arguing over a
variety of moral issues (not only sexuality), engaging in spiritual
direction and the practices of private prayer. Without this, we
shan't be in a good position to assess whether it's the same religion; and we are very likely to be assuming that what we take for
granted is the norm for a whole church or family of churches.

The books in this series are attempts to do some of this 'watching' – not approaching the question of identity in the abstract
but trying to discern how Anglicans identify themselves in their
actual life together, locally and globally. I'd like to think that
they might challenge some of the more unhelpful clichés that can
be thrown around in debate, the stereotypes used by both Global
South and Global North about each other. If it is true that – as I
have sometimes argued in other places – true interfaith dialogue
only begins as you watch the other when their faces are turned

to God, this must be true a fortiori in the Christian context. And I hope that some of these essays will allow a bit of that sort of watching. If they do, they will have helped us turn away from the lethal temptation to talk always about others when our backs are turned to them (and to God).

We all know that simply mapping the plurality of what Anglicans do is not going to answer the basic question, of course. But it is a necessary discipline for our spiritual health. It is in the light of this that we can begin to think through the broader theological issues. Let's say for the sake of argument that church communities in diverse contexts with diverse convictions about some of the major issues of the day do as a matter of bare fact manage to acknowledge each other as Anglican disciples of Jesus Christ to the extent that they are able to share some resources in theological training and diaconal service: the task then is to try and tease out what – as a matter of bare fact – makes them recognizable to each other. Not yet quite theology, but a move towards it, and above all a move away from mythologies and projections.

If I had to sum up some of my own convictions about Anglican identity, I should, I think, have to begin with the fact that, at the beginning of the English Reformation, there was a widespread agreement that Catholic unity was secured not by any external structures alone but by the faithful ministration of Word and Sacrament – 'faithful' in the sense of unadulterated by mediaeval agendas about supernatural priestly power or by the freedom of a hierarchical Church to add new doctrinal refinements to the deposit of faith. Yet as this evolved a little further, the Reformers in Britain turned away from a second-generation Calvinism which would have alarmed Calvin himself and which argued for a wholly literal application of biblical law to the present times and the exclusion from church practice of anything not contained in the plain words of Scripture. Gradually the significance of a continuous ministry in the historic style came more into focus as a vehicle of mutual recognition, eventually becoming the straightforward appeal to apostolic episcopal succession often thought to be a central characteristic of the Anglican tradition.

The blend of concern for ordered ministry (and thus ordered worship), freedom from an uncritical affirmation of hierarchical ecclesiastical authority, with the appeal to Scripture at the heart of this, and the rooted belief that the forms of common worship were the most important clues about what was held to be recognizably orthodox teaching – this blend or fusion came to define the Anglican ethos in a growing diversity of cultural contexts. Catholic, yes, in the sense of seeing the Church today as responsible to its history and to the gifts of God in the past, even those gifts given to people who have to be seen as in some ways in error. Reformed, yes, in the sense that the principle remains of subjecting the state of the Church at any given moment to the judgement of Scripture – though not necessarily therefore imagining that Scripture alone offers the answer to every contemporary question. And running through the treatment of these issues, a further assumption that renewal in Christ does not abolish but fulfils the long- frustrated capacities of human beings: that we are set free to sense and to think the texture of God's Wisdom in the whole of creation and at the same time to see how it is itself brought to fulfilment in the cross of Jesus.

This is the kind of definition that a sympathetic reading of the first two Anglican centuries might suggest. It certainly has implications for where we find the centre for such a definition in our own day. But the point is that it is a historical argument, not one from first principles; or rather, the principles emerge as the history is traced. Once again, it is about careful watching – not as an excuse for failing to look for a real theological centre but as a discipline of discerning the gifts that have actually been given to us as Anglicans.

Not many, I suspect, would seriously want to argue that the Anglican identity can be talked about without reference to Catholic creeds and ministry, or to think that a 'family' of churches can be spoken of without spelling out at least the essential family resemblances in terms of what Christ has uniquely done and what Christ continues to do in his Body through Word and Sacrament. But to understand how this does and does not, can and cannot, work, we need the kind of exact and imaginative study

that this series offers us. I hope that many readers will take the
trouble to work with the grain of such investigations, so that
our life in the Communion (and in communion itself in its fullest
sense, the communion of the Holy Spirit) will be enriched as well
as calmed, and challenged as well as reinforced.

+*Rowan Cantuar:*
from Lambeth Palace, Advent 2009

ABOUT THE CONTRIBUTORS

The Revd Professor Mark Chapman is the Vice-Principal of Ripon College Cuddesdon and Reader in Modern Theology at the University of Oxford.

The Rt Revd Suheil S. Dawani, Bishop of Jerusalem, is the fourth Arab Anglican bishop and the fourteenth Anglican bishop in Jerusalem.

The Revd Ian T. Douglas Ph.D. is the Angus Dun Professor of Mission and World Christianity at the Episcopal Divinity School in Cambridge, Massachusetts and a member of the Design Group for the 2008 Lambeth Conference.

The Rt Revd C. Christopher Epting is the Deputy for Ecumenical and Inter-religious Relations for The Episcopal Church, United States.

The Rt Revd Clive Handford is the Assistant Bishop of Ripon and Leeds, England, and was formerly Bishop of Cyprus and the Gulf and Presiding Bishop of Jerusalem and the Middle East.

The Rt Revd John William Hind is the Bishop of Chichester, Church of England.

The Rt Revd Dr Michael Jackson is the Bishop of Clogher, Church of Ireland and chairperson of the Network for Inter

Faith Concerns across the Anglican Communion (NIFCON) Management Group.

The Revd Canon Professor Martyn Percy is the Principal of Ripon College Cuddesdon.

The Rt Revd Dr Stephen Pickard is the Assistant Bishop of Adelaide, Anglican Church of Australia.

The Rt Revd Geoffrey Rowell is the Bishop of Gibraltar in Europe and Vice-Chair of the Inter-Anglican Standing Commission of Ecumenical Relations (IASCER).

The Rt Revd Dr Johannes T. Seoka is the Bishop of Pretoria, Anglican Church of Southern Africa.

The Rt Revd Dr James Tengatenga is the Bishop of Southern Malawi, Church of the Province of Central Africa, and Chair of the Anglican Consultative Council.

The Rt Revd Saw John Wilme is the Bishop of Taungoo, Church of the Province of Myanmar (Burma).

The Rt Revd N. Thomas Wright is the Bishop of Durham, Church of England.

FOREWORD

Take up this tome with a touch of restraint – meditate on its contents, rather than devour the whole at a single sitting. Be an Anglican, for God's sake, and the sake of a world much in need of patient confidence that God's will is being worked out in the messiness of our human and godly communion.

Bishops are the subject of much of this repast, with encouragement that they be homely, in the ancient spiritual sense of Julian's wisdom. Bishops must be well-grounded in the midst of this Christian family, in their capacity to speak insightfully to the members as well as prophetically to those both within and outside. Bishops are leaders and servants at once, both sheep and shepherds, and likely to fail if they ignore that tense paradox.

Anglicans are particularly called to live in that tense and undecided place, making room for the more pedestrian family members as well as the ones some find outré. The branches on the Christ-vine bear a variety of fruit, some of which seems tastier than others. The bishop's task is to feed the sheep, and not all of them will flourish on identical diets. Jesus sent out the disciples to eat what was set before them, rather than settle at only one kind of table, and he modeled that behavior even when the meal seemed bitter and deadly.

Martyn Percy bids us remember the ascetic virtue of patience, the Anglican charism of undecidability, and forbearance from exclusion on grounds of apparent error. God's spirit will continue to speak in the space between. The bishop's vocation is to speak for and into that space, challenging all parties toward mutual courage and confidence about their differences as well as the common graft they share. There is little possibility of true communion if the vine's various fruitful gifts are hidden under paper bags or bushel baskets or sheltered in glass bottles. One crop may be produced in that way, but the fruit is likely to be sterile. Abundant life is messy – it's created, organic, incarnate, and diverse – like Anglicans – and it depends on cross-fertilization.

Our common vocation is to heal the world, to reconcile its division, to feed the hungry, liberate prisoners, and nurse the sick. We do the work in the name of the one who came among us, human and divine, to lead the way past death's finality. Anglicans can challenge the world to follow, if we can remember who we are, and claim our vocation to bless and flourish, in the midst of our unresolved messiness – in some quarters known as contextual diversity for the sake of the Gospel. Enjoy this multiple-course banquet!

Katharine Jefferts Schori,
Presiding Bishop, The Episcopal Church

EDITORS' PREFACE

The writers of these Lambeth Essays were invited to extend the work of the Lambeth Conference 2008: to take the themes of the Conference into every corner of the Anglican Communion and to make the themes accessible for grassroots conversation and reflection. So, we have theological reflections from a few of the Anglican scholars and leaders who attended the 2008 conference. Because the themes are not disembodied concepts, removed from the faith journey and life experience of each delegate to the Lambeth Conference, we needed individuals to reflect on their moment with a particular theme. The writers come from across the landscape of Anglicanism and from a wide spectrum of theological perspectives. We sought in our writers a cross-section and a culturally diverse swath of our Communion – for we are many voices with many viewpoints.

These reflections draw on the daily schedule of the Lambeth Conference and the various themes that shaped the Episcopal discourse. The first day and the first theme after the beginning retreat by the archbishop in the hallowed space of Canterbury Cathedral were about the bishop and Anglican identity. Thereafter, there were days devoted to the bishop as evangelist; the bishop as activist with a heart for social justice; the bishop as embodiment of God's mission; the bishop as environmentalist; and the bishop as conversationalist with other faiths. Final sessions looked at the abuse of power, what it means to live 'under' Scripture, the challenge of human sexuality and deliberations about an Anglican Covenant and the Windsor Process. No bishop came to these themes without personal knowledge and personal concern. These essays reflect the fact that Lambeth themes are the daily care and work of those who lead the Anglican Communion.

The Lambeth Conference is a decennial gathering of Anglican bishops, one order of the ministry of the baptized who converse about the larger Church and its ministry and mission. Twenty-first-century Anglicanism cannot be shaped by bishops only or by a bishop-centred conference. So, we have sought theological reflections from Anglican scholars and leaders who attended the Conference because we want to encourage conversation about the Lambeth themes in the provinces, dioceses and parishes of the Communion. It is well to know what the bishops thought about proclaiming the Good News. But what do the faithful in the pew or on the grass mat believe about evangelism? The study questions at the end of the book will help all who read this book to go deeper and to live with the themes of Lambeth 2008. The themes of Lambeth 2008 are our themes, and this book brings them to us.

At Lambeth 2008 small groups were referred to as *indabas* which means 'respectful engagement' in Zulu. It must have been the hope of the framers of Lambeth 2008 that the Conference itself would become an *indaba* writ large. If that is to be a reality, then the 'big tent' where the bishops met at Lambeth must become an ever bigger tent as the Communion gathers in small groups across this globe to reflect on God and God's Church and the hopes Anglicans have for a Communion frayed, strong, small and very large.

Special thanks are due to all those who helped with this project, especially Leslie Steffensen, of the Center for Anglican Communion Studies, and Dr Jenny Gaffin of Ripon College Cuddesdon.

Mark Chapman
Barney Hawkins
Ian Markham
Martyn Percy

Easter 2009

INTRODUCTION

Mark Chapman

The Lambeth Conference of 2008 was not like any of its predecessors. It was a conference established on the principle of listening rather than speaking. It did not issue any resolutions, and it made virtually no decisions. Instead it offered the opportunity for extended discussion and listening in relatively intimate groups – the focus was on Bible study and what were called *indaba* groups. All that formally emerged at the end of the Conference was a lengthy set of reflections which came out of these groups. These offered a summary of the issues that had been discussed through the course of the fortnight as bishops from across the globe gathered together to listen and learn from one another. The Archbishop of Canterbury was only too aware of the politicking of the 1998 Conference, as well as the effects that making controversial resolutions had had on the stability of the Anglican Communion. He deliberately aimed at a very different sort of gathering in which voices and views could be aired in an atmosphere of trust and patience.

This meant that the Lambeth Design Group, which was charged with setting the agenda for the meeting, consequently developed a method which would 'enable the bishops to meet in real encounter in a way which would not be dominated by political positioning or parliamentary process'. This was to be achieved by the *indaba* process, which was based on a Zulu method of conflict resolution:

> [It is a] gathering for purposeful discussion. It is both a process and method of engagement as we listen to one another concerning challenges that face our community and by extension the Anglican Communion. An *indaba* first and foremost acknowledges that there are issues that need to be addressed effectively to foster on-going communal living. Originally, in the Zulu context, these would include issues which affected the whole of the community. In our case it is issues which affect the whole Communion as reflected in our daily themes. In *Indaba*, we must be aware of these challenges (issues) without immediately trying to resolve them one way or the other. We meet and converse, ensuring that everyone has a voice, and contributes (in our case, praying that it might be under the guidance of the Holy Spirit) and that the issues at hand are fully defined and understood by all.[1]

The point of meeting is less about reaching a definitive settlement or ending a controversy – instead it is about clarification, about thinking through the issues that divide, which are so closely related to the different contexts in which Anglicanism has taken root over the last 300 years or so. All this requires a far deeper sense of listening than many Christians are used to; and it requires a vulnerability and a willingness to be changed that many in the Church – perhaps especially bishops – find remarkably difficult.

From a pragmatic point of view, this sort of method is probably all that could be hoped for given the constraints of Anglican history, especially over the past ten years. Obviously, something different could have been tried, but, as the archbishop said in his opening presidential address to the Conference:

> Quite a few people have said that the new ways we're suggesting of doing our business are an attempt to avoid tough decisions and have the effect of replacing substance with process. To such people, I'd simply say, 'How effective have the

old methods really been?' Earlier Lambeth Conferences issued weighty reports and passed scores of resolutions . . . no-one would say they have been a waste of time, because they still embody a lot of careful thinking and planning. Yet not much of this material attempts to convey what was different about meeting in a prolonged time of prayer and fellowship as we always do at these Conferences. And as for resolutions: if you look at the resolutions that have been passed since 1867, you'll find many of them, on really important subjects, have never been acted on. At the very first Lambeth Conference, the assembled bishops passed a resolution asking for some kind of supreme canonical court in the Communion which could settle points of dispute in provinces. What happened to that resolution, I wonder? Often we have passed a motion but not thought what would be necessary to make it take effect.[2]

To avoid a repeat performance, something very different was required.

What I want to do in this introduction is to think through this process – which leads in two directions. First, I will ask how we understand the Anglican Communion as catholic – what sort of model of catholicity do we have and how is this affected by Anglican history? This leads to the related question of how the notion of catholicity has been changed by the 2008 Conference. Second, I will look in detail at what sort of bishops are required in a reconceived Catholicism that moves beyond what I call the 'contained Catholicism' of the Anglican tradition. Ultimately this question leads on to the far more important issue of what Christianity is really about, and where its centre is to be found. First, however, I will discuss what I consider some aspects of Anglican history which provide a crucial backdrop to any renewed quest for catholicity.

The Anglican problem

The sorts of issues that the archbishop highlighted in his opening address stem in part from the particular historical circumstances of the development of the Anglican Communion. Even though there has been a gradual creation of 'instruments of unity' to bind the Anglican Communion together from the time of the first Lambeth Conference of 1867, the structures of authority that have developed are still extraordinarily weak. The four instruments that have been established over the years are (obviously) the Archbishop of Canterbury (established in AD 597), the Lambeth Conference (1867), the Anglican Consultative Council (1968), and the Primates' Meeting (1978). Even though they have claimed more authority in recent years they still have no legal authority over the constituent churches. Unlike the Roman Catholic Church, which has a clear set of canonical regulations between the churches of the different nations, none of the instruments of unity has any juridical force across provincial boundaries at all. The only sanction is expulsion from the councils, although this has seldom been used, even through the bitter conflicts of the past ten years. What this means is that all that remains for any of these instruments is a limited amount of moral pressure – even if some would prefer expulsion to be rather more frequently applied.

The history of the Anglican Communion and the Church that spawned it reveals the main source of the problem. When Thomas Cromwell declared boldly in 1534 that 'This realm of England is an Empire' and Henry VIII made rather rapid use of that sort of imperial power in matters ecclesiastical, this meant that the Church *in* England became the Church *of* England. What had hitherto been a frequently troublesome couple of provinces on the edge of western Christendom mutated into a form of religion completely bounded and under the control of the absolute sovereign. This meant that, at least at the beginning of the Church of England, it was impossible for Anglicanism (although the word is anachronistic) (Chapman: 2006, pp. 4–5) to be anything other than a local phenomenon. The Church might have continued to claim catholicity, but it was a form of catholicity limited to the realm of England. Despite the many conflicts between Church and state through the Middle Ages, medieval Christendom was the global phenomenon *par excellence*. Following the many reformations of the national churches of northern Europe, global Catholicism was divided into many local communities – in the German-speaking territories, for instance, there was a church for every petty princedom, some Lutheran, some Reformed and some Roman Catholic.

Although it is not fair to say that the Church of England was completely isolated, it is nevertheless true that one of its principal defining characteristics was that it was not Roman Catholic. In other words, *rejection* of Roman Catholicism, and particularly the papacy, was fundamental to the origin of the English Reformation. The great texts of the early Anglican writers are often exercises in anti-Roman Catholic polemic. For instance, John Jewel (1522–71), Bishop of Salisbury and the first Anglican apologist of the Elizabethan years, tried to prove the Church of England was more catholic than the Church of Rome, and more properly located in the Church of the Fathers. 'As for our doctrine,' he wrote, 'which we might rightlier call Christ's catholic doctrine, it is so far off from new, that God, who is above all most ancient, and the Father of our Lord Jesus Christ, hath left the same unto us in the Gospel, in the prophets' and apostles' works, being monuments of greatest age. So that no man can now think our doctrine to be new, unless the same think either the prophets' faith, or the Gospel, or else Christ himself to be new' (Jewel: 1845–50, vol. 1 p. 39). For Jewel, the Church of England was the true heir of the past, since it had been purged of the worst excesses of the middle ages.

Jewel faced many charges from his Roman Catholic opponents. For instance, he responded to those who had accused him of failing to acknowledge the role of councils in the formulation of doctrine, by claiming that nothing had been done in the Reformation without the authority of councils. Indeed, the lay synod of the Church, parliament itself, had ratified the actions of the reformers:

> Yet truly we do not despise councils, assemblies, and conferences of bishops and learned men; neither have we done that we have done altogether without bishops or without a council.

The matter hath been treated in *open parliament*, with long consultation, and before a notable synod and convocation. (Jewel: 1845–50, vol. 1 p. 47)

At the same time, however, councils had only a limited authority. As Jewel wrote: 'Whatsoever it be, the truth of the gospel of Jesus Christ dependeth not upon the councils' (Jewel: 1845–50, vol. 3 p. 54).

What I want to stress from this brief discussion of the early theology of the Church of England is threefold: first, the Church of England defined itself as a catholic church in continuity with the past, but at the same time it did not recognize any authority beyond that exercised within the realm of England. While the ultimate authority in the Church of England might be the gospel of Jesus Christ, there could be no appeal to 'any foreign prince, person, state or potentate, spiritual or temporal' in the interpretation or implementation of that gospel.[3] Second, however, the synodical aspect of the Church of England was always central – in its early years it was certainly not a church ruled over by bishops. Its sources of authority were far more complex and often highly contested. A significant degree of power was exercised by the laity in parliament: indeed, conflicts between king, bishops and parliament over control of the Church were a principal cause of the British civil wars of the 1640s. Third, the authority of councils has always been ambiguous in Anglicanism: echoing Article XXI of the Thirty-Nine Articles which sees councils as 'an assembly of men', and therefore open to error, Jewel is clear that there is always a degree of provisionality in their rulings.

The Church of England expressed what can be called a kind of 'contained catholicity' – that is, it considered itself catholic, but such Catholicism was expressed more temporally than spatially. As the historian Norman Sykes said:

The validity of the Anglican position depends upon the recognition of the right of national churches to fashion their own doctrine, discipline, and organization, and of the right of the laity to participate in the definition of matters of faith and order. (Sykes: 1936, p. 301)

In other words, it was united with the Church of the fathers and stood in continuity with the Church of St Augustine, but it was not connected in the same way with churches across the channel. It is thus not without some justification to see the essence of the Reformation in completely independent, national churches, rather than in any conception of an international 'communion'. Although there were various pan-Protestant alliances in the sixteenth and seventeenth centuries in which the English Church participated – most obviously at the Synod of Dort in 1618–19 – for most of the time the English Church existed independently of other churches. And it even lacked the obvious confessional identity which united the Lutheran or Calvinist churches on the continent.

Without trying to cram in 400 years of history of missions into a few sentences, it is this idea of 'contained catholicity' which became the key principle of the Anglican doctrine of the Church as it expanded overseas. Although there were obviously many connections with the English Crown in the early years of missionary endeavour (Strong: 2007 and Jacob: 1997), the example of the American Church clearly displays this form of independent ecclesiology (Doll: 2000): for instance, the Crown could have no authority over a church when it had completely lost control over the American colonies. What was rapidly adopted at the General Convention in 1789 was a democratic constitution modelled on the new political arrangements for the USA – the Church remained synodically governed by a house of deputies and a house of bishops. What they governed was a church which was as equally independent as the Church of England from any other church.

By the end of the nineteenth century there were many separate churches through the Anglican Communion governed by their own constitutions, often with quite different structures from the Church of England. While most were still united with the mother Church in terms of culture and even though England still provided most of the leaders, the different national churches were independent of direct control: gone were the days when a colonial bishop, like Bishop Colenso, could appeal to the British Courts. The Lambeth Conference was summoned by Archbishop Longley in 1867 partly in response to a number of calls to work out how these newly independent churches were to be regulated. Although there was a clamour for firm leadership and strong decision-making powers, what emerged was quite the opposite. Longley, and his successors through the early Conferences, resisted centralization (Sachs: 1993; Stephenson: 1967 and 1978; Chapman, 2008) – while resolutions were issued they had no legal authority unless the constituent churches decided to act upon them. Besides, in most churches the bishop's authority was restricted by synodical government. Through much of the nineteenth and twentieth centuries the bonds of affection between the churches survived through imperial and colonial links – the Anglican Communion was characterized by a vague sense of Englishness (and to a lesser extent Americanness); English forms of worship and English hymn books continued to be used; and, even though the identities of the different missionary societies shaped the new churches, there were still enough connections for a strong set of family resemblances.

In more recent years, however, many factors have meant that things have changed rapidly. Among these one might include the end of colonialism; the reaction to the former colonizers; the decline of the numerical strength of Anglicanism in the developed world; and the indigenization of leadership. All of these mean that the different 'contained catholic' churches have developed separately and in sometimes contradictory ways. And without a firm central authority it is sometimes difficult to see precisely what binds Anglican churches together: in ecumenical times they can no longer rely for their identity on being against Roman Catholicism (or Puritanism) as in the early days of the independent Church of England. They might still be 'temporally catholic' in the sense that they see themselves in continuity with the Church of the Fathers, but it is far more difficult to locate spatial continuity with other Anglican churches, which might appear very different. The old liturgical and doctrinal identities have gradually been eroded through contextualization and adaptation.

It is consequently easy to see the Anglican Communion as a collection of 'contained catholic' churches, each relating primarily to its own context – from Kenya to Mexico, and from Singapore to New Zealand. But it is not so easy to speak of the Anglican Communion as *a* church. And yet in the contemporary world, with instant communication, this means that the tension between international networks and local independence can be stretched to breaking point. What goes on in New Hampshire is no longer restricted to the pages of the *Concord Monitor* but can be known immediately in Lagos and every other city across the world. Whether we like it or not the Anglican Communion is no longer simply a collection of more or less loosely united national churches – it has networks of interaction and interdependence that make it some sort of catholic church rather than a loose federation of 'contained catholic' churches. The question that has emerged in recent years, however, is precisely what sort of wider catholicity can regulate the 'contained catholic churches'. This has become especially pressing after the 1998 Lambeth Conference and the resulting Windsor process. In other words, if the Anglican Communion is a type of catholic church, then what does that catholicity look like? How can a collection of 'contained catholic' churches be held together in a catholic network, that is, in an Anglican Church worldwide? Those are the questions I shall address through the remainder of this introduction in relation to Lambeth 2008.

Models of catholicity

While obviously the presenting issue behind recent Anglican disputes was the compatibility of homosexual practice with ordination and the related issue of the use of Scripture, the ecclesiological question of the relationship between the national church and the international communion remains fundamental. By its very nature as something transnational, catholicity refuses to be contained in practice within the confines of the provincial churches. For some Anglicans it is clear that the best way forward is to define Anglicanism more rigidly and prescriptively and ensure that churches subscribe to a set of doctrinal propositions. Many of the approximately 289 bishops who met in Jerusalem at the Global Anglican Future Conference shortly before the Lambeth Conference were evidently dissatisfied with the slow process towards an Anglican Covenant or agreement between the churches.[4] In his opening address at the Conference, Peter Akinola, primate of Nigeria (with Peter Jenson, Archbishop of Sydney, joint leader of the movement), spoke in the language of spiritual warfare:

> Our beloved Anglican Communion must be rescued from the manipulation of those who have denied the gospel and its power to transform and to save; those who have departed from the scripture and the faith once and for all delivered to the saints, from those who are proclaiming a new gospel, which really is no gospel at all (Gal. 1). In the wisdom and strength God supplies we must rescue what is left of the Church from error of the apostates . . .
>
> We are here because we know that in God's providence GAFCON will liberate and set participants free from spiritual bondage which TEC [The Episcopal Church] and its allies champion. Having survived the inhuman physical slavery of the 19th century, the political slavery called colonialism of the 20th century, and the developing world's economic enslavement, we cannot, we dare not allow ourselves and the millions we represent to be kept in a religious and spiritual dungeon.
> . . . A sizeable part of the Communion is in error and not a few are apostate; is the Communion correctable from within or must it be from without?[5]

In equally powerful language he claimed that the instruments of unity did little more than promote disunity, and that the strong words of the resolutions made by the Lambeth Conference and the primates had been ignored and trivialized by the official structures of the Anglican Communion.

After the Jerusalem meeting a statement was issued which suggested that the only solution was either to make use of the existing instruments of unity to expel the errant churches, or to set up a network within the Anglican Communion of true churches. The statement saw the spread of liberal values as a form of neo-colonialism that had to be resisted at all costs:

> Despite numerous meetings and reports to and from the 'Instruments of Unity,' no effective action has been taken, and the bishops of these unrepentant churches are welcomed to Lambeth 2008. To make matters worse, there has been a failure to honour promises of discipline, the authority of the Primates' Meeting has been undermined and the Lambeth Conference has been structured so as to avoid any hard decisions. We can only come to the devastating conclusion that we are a global Communion with a colonial structure.

The Fellowship of Confessing Anglicans, which was established at the Conference, is clearly a call for some sort of clearly defined group, either inside or outside the wider Anglican Communion. It was to be founded on subscription to a set of teachings based upon a particular way of reading the Bible, which 'is to be translated, read, preached, taught and obeyed in its plain and canonical sense, respectful of the church's historic and consensual reading'. It is no accident that the framers of the statement drew explicitly on language derived from the Confessing Church of 1930s Germany which resisted the Nazi regime. The statement also suggests that the (so-called) orthodox primates should begin to act against the churches which have strayed from orthodoxy: 'We reject the authority of those churches and leaders who have denied the orthodox faith in word or deed.'

What the Gafcon bishops called for was a new structure to control membership through a far tighter definition of catholicity. For them, catholicity is not restricted to national boundaries, but is modelled on doctrinal purity. Ironically, perhaps, their goal is far closer to the tightly controlled curial model of modern Roman Catholicism. Thus they claim:

> We recognize the desirability of territorial jurisdiction for provinces and dioceses of the Anglican Communion, except in those areas where churches and leaders are denying the orthodox faith or are preventing its spread, and in a few areas for which overlapping jurisdictions are beneficial for historical or cultural reasons.
>
> We thank God for the courageous actions of those Primates and provinces who have offered orthodox oversight to churches under false leadership, especially in North and South America. The actions of these Primates have been a positive response to pastoral necessities and mission opportunities. We believe that such actions will continue to be necessary and we support them in offering help around the world.
>
> We believe this is a critical moment when the Primates' Council will need to put in place structures to lead and support the church. In particular, we believe the time is now ripe for the formation of a province in North America for the federation currently known as Common Cause Partnership to be recognized by the Primates' Council.

Interactive pluralism

A very different model of catholicity was tried at the Lambeth Conference a few weeks later. As I noted at the beginning, the archbishop sought to encourage a deep sense of listening to establish the conditions for a vision of the church based on understanding rather than condemnation and exclusion. What was attempted through the *indaba* process was a form of catholicity which resembles what the archbishop has called (in a different context) 'interactive pluralism' (Williams: 2000, p. 174). The basic process is simple. Many different views are brought to the table of fellowship; voices come together not necessarily to find consensus, but instead to understand each other better, to converse and to share and learn from another – and in such dialogue the bonds of communion are deepened. As with the sort of democratic politics that can exist without a strong executive power – which the archbishop has promoted in many speeches[6] – so with the Anglican Communion. It has to be based on a willingness among its members to participate, to open up to others, even to those with whom they vigorously disagree. Decisions will emerge (if they emerge at all) as participants voluntarily agree to certain constraints on unilateral action. 'Contained Catholicism' is thereby constrained by some sense of spatial catholicity. In a situation where authority has to be negotiated and where there is effectively no coercive power (as with other voluntary organizations), the process of consensus can work only if there is a relinquishing of certain freedoms through the desire to belong to a spatially extensive catholic church. Coming together in deep listening is thus not simply about tolerating difference, but about exploring and understanding that difference, and drawing it into one's own decision-making structures.

This method relates closely to Williams' recent discussions of multiculturalism.[7] In May 2008, for instance, he spoke in an interview about the nature of community cohesion in modern Britain, which seems equally relevant to the problems of the Anglican Communion:

> You have to start with what cohesion means, and look at the difference between cohesion and consensus and between cohesion and homogenization. I'd like to think that cohesion allowed that dimension I have sometimes called 'interactive pluralism' where you have communities that are sufficiently robust in themselves to engage with one another and challenge each other while the state stands by to prevent this degenerating into violence. But to see cohesion as a situation where no one is allowed to challenge anyone else is a sad view of social life. We should be able to do better than that.[8]

The Catholic Church might seem to resemble that sort of state – its role is both negative and positive. It serves to prevent the different groups (in this case national churches, or ecclesiastical parties) degenerating into violence while at the same time promoting cohesion – or in Christian vocabulary, *koinonia* (communion). This understanding is also remarkably close to Rowan Williams' understanding of inter-religious dialogue:

> The goal of any specific moment of inter-faith encounter is thus – presumably – to find a way of working together towards a mode of human operation, mutual challenge and mutual nurture, which does not involve the triumph of one theory or one institution or one culture, but which is in some way unified by relation to that form of human liberty and maturity before God made concrete in Jesus. To put it slightly differently, and perhaps more traditionally, the Christian goal in engaging with other traditions is the formation of children of God after the likeness of Christ . . . pluralism is not limitless. (Is there any pluralism that is?) It involves resistance to the homogenization of human beings – *cultural* resistance, in other words, and *political* resistance, to the forces in our world that make for the reduction of persons and personal communities to units in large-scale, determined processes, resistance to the power of the universal market or the omnipotent state . . . the fullness of Christ is what defines the most comprehensive future for humankind. (Williams: 2000, pp. 174–7)

Resistance to homogenization is coupled with an acknowledgement that all people – Christian and non-Christian alike – are to be formed into the likeness of Christ. This means learning from the outsider, from the one who is different.

Even in theology, Williams has sought to learn through listening to other voices which have often been suppressed by the tradition: indeed, he sees the whole theological task as a process of communication with other voices through history and in the present day. Theology is something done in dialogue. Williams writes in the introduction to a collection of essays:

> The assumption is that this or that intellectual idiom not only offers a way into fruitful conversation with the current envi-

ronment but also that the unfamiliar idiom may uncover aspects of the deposit of belief hitherto unexamined. In fact, it involves a considerable act of trust in the theological tradition, a confidence that the fundamental categories of belief are robust enough to survive the drastic experience of immersion in other ways of constructing and construing the world.

But there can come a point here where the passage through unfamiliar media of thought provokes a degree of crisis: is what is emerging actually identical or at least continuous with what has been believed and articulated? (Williams: 2000, p. xiv)

Even though there are boundaries, it is only at the end of the process that the difficult decisions have to be made and not at the beginning; only at the end of the process is there a need to make a judgement, a crisis.

Rowan Williams' theology of the Lambeth Conference

Throughout the Lambeth Conference, Rowan Williams similarly emphasized the need to listen – and he spent much time wrestling with the issue of what sort of conditions were required for deep listening to take place. His retreat addresses to the bishops, which were given over the first weekend, offered reflections on being united in Christ, the absolute need for God's grace, but also on the need to listen, both to one another and to Christ, the one who 'both judges us and heals us' (*First Address*). He stressed the nature of Christian power which was to be found through the weakness displayed in the utter emptying of Christ: being a bishop is about following in this path, thereby 'leading, clearing the way, making it possible for us to go where otherwise we could not' (*Fifth Address*). Bishops thus exercise a form of authority that cannot simply affirm others, but which frequently challenges people 'to change, to be converted and to grow':

We would all like to be good and reliable allies, and yet God says, 'You're never just the prisoner of one person, one agenda, one cause, one nation, one political perspective. You are always the person who has that "something more" to add in the name of the body of the Christ who gathers.'

The challenge facing bishops is to exercise this ministry of 'something more': it is an act of interpretation in the light of the New Creation:

> It would be much simpler if one could say of the Church (as people sometimes like to say) that it is an association of people who agree about every item in the following list, or (as has often been said in the past, not least by the Church of England) that we are the church of this nation and that's really all that matters to us.

But for Williams it is simply not like that. There will always be dispute and division, and the role of bishops is to ask the awkward questions about 'uncritical kinds of belonging'. The bishop is a sign of unity, but not the sort of unity expressed by the impartial chairman; and neither is it the sort of unity that sees the bishop as a charismatic on a Monday, an Anglo-Catholic on a Tuesday, and a liberal on a Wednesday. Instead the bishop is a sign of unity in a 'rather different and a rather deeper way'. Williams thus asks:

> What if we are meant to be a sign of that unity of the new humanity in which there are no defensive boundaries between the life and the pain of diverse people and communities? What if we are meant to be signs of that unity, where, in Christ and through the Spirit, human lives flow together to announce God's glory?
> When we say we believe in 'one, holy, catholic and apostolic Church' surely we mean more by that 'one' than the bare fact (if it is a fact, which it isn't) that there is just one Christian institution. We mean, surely, a oneness which is bound up with the holiness, the apostolic quality, the catholic quality, a oneness that is about quality of relation and of life. And if we as

bishops are to be signs of unity, I believe that is the nature of the unity we have to show. And that is why our ministry and mission is a sign of hope and a challenge for conversion to the whole world around. (*Second Address*)

Here there is an explicit linking of the role of bishop as the sign of the new humanity with a form of catholicity that expresses the relationality that comes from new life in Christ. This does not amount to a simple consensus, but to a way of living so that lives flow into one another – and that is achieved through deep listening.

According to Williams 'the bishop is a linguist' who learns how to speak a language, obeying the rules so that communication occurs. This involves

> listening for the nuances, listening for the hidden music in what someone says or does, listening sometimes for what's beneath the surface as well as what is immediately in front of us. It's a tough experience, and it doesn't happen quickly.

While ultimately this act of listening requires us first to listen to the language that emanates from God's Word, at the same time it is heard in the context of listening to the other voices around us. Again this is modelled on Jesus, who listens to those around him by 'learning our language, listening to our needs, answering our hunger'. Williams goes on:

> I don't know if this makes sense to you, but I'm often struck in the gospels by how Jesus says to those in need, 'What do you want me to do for you?' It's as if Jesus is saying, 'Tell me what to do, and I will obey you as I obey my Father. Tell me what your need is, and in giving my love to you I will be obeying my Father.' So that Jesus' humility before the needs of the suffering, sinful world is absolutely at one with his obedience and humility before God, his source, his Father. To be a Christlike stranger is to be listening for the true need around us and to hold that together with our listening to God.

This means that listening is something that involves interpretation. Williams likens this to a 'stereophonic capacity'. The bishop – and this is presumably equally true for all others involved in any form of Christian discipleship – 'listens with one ear to the word of God, and the other to the languages of those among whom he or she ministers. And somehow the messages come to the one centre of heart and brain, and we live under the law of Christ.' At the same time, however, the bishop may well be reduced to silence through the process of listening out for God's word:

> The bishop whose ministry is centred on the Eucharist, performed with the wholeness of the Church in mind, will be a bishop who is silent in respect of many of the claims and pressures that are around, holding still so that God's word – not the bishop's – can come through. Open, therefore to the differences, the difficulties in letting God's word through, but also beginning, maturing, ending in the quiet that allows God to be God and doesn't impose the agenda of the individual and their fleshly nature. (*Third Address*)

That balance between listening, silence and speaking, it seems to me, is at the heart of the form of catholicity envisaged by the archbishop – and tried out at Lambeth:

> I've said that as bishops-in-communion we need to be a kind of church together. We need to model sharing, honesty and common prayer. That means, I believe, that faithfulness to our Anglican identity is faithfulness to each other as much as it is faithfulness to some norm or standard of teaching: the two go together. And it is in the growth and deepening of faithfulness to each other, in our shared, collegial exercise of Episcopal ministry, that we build up our confidence. In the planning and imagining of this conference, I and others have spoken from time to time of the need to restore confidence in our life as a communion and in its structures. The word 'confidence' has the same central significance as 'fidelity'; they're both in different ways about *fides*, about faith and trust. As we discover

a real faithfulness to each other, I believe we discover the true confidence we most deeply need. We recognize in one another the same faith and the same prayer, and we communicate with each other trustfully, not suspiciously. (*Fourth Address*)

Being Anglican is thus not about following formularies but about discovering the living way of Christ.

In his third retreat address, the archbishop drew on one of his heroes to explain his point – the strange and troublesome lay theologian, William Stringfellow (1928–85), whom he has frequently referred to in his writings and lectures. He takes up one of Stringfellow's leading themes, that of being a 'biblical person' as distinct from a 'religious person':

A religious person knows the words and the habits that satisfy religious demands, and can make a very time-consuming hobby or pastime of being religious. A biblical person is one caught in the spotlight of God's call and God's attention, called to obedience, called to danger, to transformed life. A religious person is perhaps a calm and relaxed person, knowing exactly what to do. A biblical person is very frightened. I'm not suggesting that the essence of being a good bishop is to be very frightened, though sometimes it does us good to be – but that to be a bishop is to be a biblical person, caught in the spotlight of God's attention, God's call, working out our future with fear and trembling because it's only when we know something of the fear of being caught in the spotlight of God's attention that we know the meaning of the words, 'Fear not!', which Jesus Christ addresses to his disciples. (*Third Address*)

In a book published in 1967, in a passage about the interpretation of the Bible, Stringfellow emphasized the absolute centrality of listening in becoming a 'biblical person'. He wrote:

Listening is a rare happening among human beings. You cannot listen to the word another is speaking if you are preoccupied with your appearance or impressing the other, or if you are trying to decide what you are going to say when the other stops talking, or if you are debating about whether the word being spoken is true or relevant or agreeable. Such matters may have their place, but only after listening to the word as the word is being uttered. Listening, in other words, is a primitive act of love, in which a person gives oneself to another's word, making oneself accessible and vulnerable to that word. (Stringfellow: 1967, pp. 15–20, cited in Dancer: 2005, p. 23)

Here, I think, is an unspoken assumption behind the archbishop's Lambeth method: love is discovered through the self-emptying vulnerability that comes through a genuine openness to the other person. Later in the same book, Stringfellow wrote of the need to be absolutely open to God's initiative. There was a need to give up

. . . all hypotheses, speculations, ideas and deductions about God – that God is not and that there is only death. When one is so naked, so helpless, so transparent, when one so utterly ceases to try to justify oneself or anyone or anything else, one first becomes vulnerable to the Word of God, which overcomes oblivion, heals deafness, restores sight and saves people from manipulation, arrogance and folly in confronting the Word of God in the Bible. When one becomes that mature as a human being one is freed to listen and at last to welcome the Word in the Bible, and one is enlightened to discern the same Word of God at work now in the world . . . Thus is established a rhythm in the Christian's life; encompassing intimacy with the Word of God in the Bible and involvement with the same Word active in the world. (Dancer: 2005, p. 26)

In a sermon entitled 'Being Biblical Persons' preached at a conference on Stringfellow, Williams had earlier developed this theme of vulnerability and living biblically. He writes:

The religious person looks at his or her one world and seeks to interpret as the secular person seeks to interpret it; to make sense. The biblical person puts himself or herself in the way of being interpreted, 'being made sense of'. The biblical person risks being vulnerable, because to put yourself in the way of being made sense of is to become vulnerable. The interpreter is the person with power, the person with the categories to organize the world. The person being interpreted is the person whose hands and heart are open to receive a very worrying and not always welcome gift, because the sense being made of us may not be the sense we would like to make. Or to put it more bluntly, the way God sees us may not be the way we would like to see ourselves. (Williams: 2005, p. 184)

Seeing bishops as biblical persons is both original and challenging: episcopacy becomes a difficult task, like walking along a tightrope. And yet this is the way of discipleship: 'living in the Church', he said while still Archbishop of Wales, 'certainly involves walking various kinds of tightropes (living as an Archbishop in the church is probably even more of a delicate acrobatic act that most)' (Williams: 2005, p. 186).

Following on from the opening retreat the archbishop went on to give a steer to the Conference in his presidential addresses: he continued to focus on the discussion of what he called a form of Anglicanism 'whose diversity is limited not by centralized control but by consent . . . since the entire church is present in every local church assembled around the Lord's table' (*First Presidential Address*). In his second address he even imagined the conversation and feelings of two different bishops from opposite sides of the globe and of the current ethical debates. Williams was able to express the hurts felt on both sides, expressing an appeal for generosity in order to listen to what was being said:

Two sets of feelings and perceptions, two appeals for generosity. For the first speaker, the cost of generosity may be accusation of compromise: you've been bought, you've been deceived by airy talk into tolerating unscriptural and unfaithful policies. For the second speaker, the cost of generosity may be accusations of sacrificing the needs of an oppressed group for the sake of a false or delusional unity, giving up a precious Anglican principle for the sake of a dangerous centralization. But there is the challenge. If both were able to hear and to respond generously, perhaps we could have something more like a conversation of equals – even something more like a Church. (*Second Presidential Address*)

Conversation required an openness and a spirit of generosity, that is, a preparedness to listen and to try to understand. Challenging his Episcopal audience he asked:

To the innovator, can we say, 'Don't isolate yourself; don't create facts on the ground that make the invitation to debate ring a bit hollow'? Can we say to the traditionalist, 'Don't invest everything in a church of pure and likeminded souls; try to understand the pastoral and human and theological issues that are urgent for those you are opposing, even if you think them deeply wrong'?

I think we perhaps can, if and only if we are captured by the vision of the true Centre, the heart of GOD out of which flows the impulse of an eternal generosity which creates and heals and promises. It is this generosity which sustains our mission and service in Our Lord's name. And it is this we are called to show to each other.

At the moment, we seem often to be threatening death to each other, not offering life. What some see as confused or reckless innovation in some provinces is felt as a body-blow to the integrity of mission and a matter of literal physical risk to Christians. (*Second Presidential Address*)

In his final presidential address, the archbishop returned to his favourite theme of inclusive pluralism: 'Beyond peaceful diversity', he claimed, 'lies Christian unity.' This was founded not on simple toleration, but on something far deeper – on the unity that adheres in Jesus Christ which was achieved not through compulsion or enforced conformity. Instead, it

... is an agreement to identify those elements in each other's lives that build trust and allow us to see each other as standing in the same Way and the same Truth, moving together in one direction and so able to enrich and support each other as fully as we can. What I am saying, in effect, is that every association of Christian individuals and groups makes some sort of 'covenant' for the sake of mutual recognition, mutual gratitude and mutual learning. (*Third Presidential Address*)

Catholicity, on this model, is rooted in Christ and expressed by all who seek to relate – or to covenant – to one another in order to listen to what Christ is saying. In this way the Anglican Communion might become

... more of a 'catholic' church in the proper sense, a church, that is, which understands its ministry and service and sacraments as united and interdependent throughout the world. That we wanted to move in such a direction would in itself be a weighty message. But it might even be a prophetic one. The vision of a global Church of interdependent communities is not the vision of an ecclesiastical world empire – or even a colonial relic . . . The global horizon of the Church matters because churches without this are always in danger of slowly surrendering to the culture around them and losing sight of their calling to challenge that culture. The Church of England was, for a long time, so involved in the structures of power in this nation that it had little to say that was properly critical: part of its awakening in the last century and a half is due to its slow but steady recognition that it had come to belong to a global fellowship.

There is thus a move away from a loose federation of 'contained catholic' churches towards a set of churches inter-related to one another and rooted and unified in a common endeavour to listen to one another and to Christ: 'Catholic faith affirms that the image of God is the same everywhere.' Williams concluded his message with reassuring words to the assembled bishops: 'what is most important is to say to you that it is your work, your patient, lively, impatient, hopeful engagement with each other that has, by God's grace, brought us where we are'.

Conclusion

It is hard to say whether the Conference was a success and it is probably far too soon to tell – but at least to those outside what seemed to be happening was a significant amount of serious listening. There were undoubtedly very many bishops who were deeply moved through hearing those from very different contexts; and there were many bishops who discovered something new about how to live as a Christian in the world. There was a tangible sense of discovery as voices unfamiliar to one another expressed the joys and pains of their different situations. There was remarkably little polarization, and a sense that this was a way worth trying. At the end of the Conference the archbishop was asked about the process of the Conference:

> I'd say that the process of the Lambeth Conference rested on a particular assumption – the assumption that Bishops needed to speak to each other in a safe place and were capable of doing it respectfully and prayerfully, first thing. Second thing is, coming out of that, the Communion, the Anglican Communion needed to know how deep the commitment was on people's part to staying together. I think we've got a bit of an answer to that. Third, I think the communion needed to know what forms of action and witness were still possible, credible for it, even in its current rather wobbly state and I think something around the March of Witness, something around a few other things that have come up has helped to answer that.

What emerged from this was a new way of being catholic – instead of coercion, centralization and control there was voluntary commitment to see others as disciples living in their different circumstances. Personal relations were established across the social, cultural and ecclesiastical divides, and at the same time there seemed a willingness to let divisive issues be transposed into a different, less anxious key.

The archbishop was asked how well he thought the Conference had gone. His answer was unequivocal:

I feel it's worked out very much as I had hoped and prayed. I think it's not evaded the difficult questions, even if it hasn't answered them in the ways that some people would have liked to answer them. But that doesn't cause me to lose too much sleep because the conference has never been an executive body that can simply make those sorts of quick fix decisions. I've actually been surprised by how much energy has been growing in the *Indaba* groups to continue the process of encounter, and I feel we've been very well served by our chaplaincy team in providing a climate of prayer and worship. People have said that they've felt the encounters have been serious and prayerful and without too much pressure – I don't think I could have prayed for more really. . . .

Sacrifice has to be accepted voluntarily, that's true. If it's imposed it's not sacrifice. That's why this remains something about consent, about what people are willing to give for the sake of the communion, and that means of course a judgement about what is worthwhile about the communion. There are those I know, who will not see that kind of unity as worth that kind of sacrifice, and that's not a judgement I want to pronounce on from high. I want to sit with people and see what it looks like to them as it evolves. But I think that the sense that there is something about the preservation of the global fellowship which is larger than any of us, has to be a factor in this. [9]

Of course nobody knows what will happen to the Anglican Communion. Perhaps – as one senior bishop is reported as saying – 'the operation was successful, but the patient died anyway'. But perhaps there is also a sense in which the Anglican Communion at this Lambeth Conference was pioneering a new way of being catholic – through a voluntary commitment to a non-coercive form of mutually shared authority. It may have been forced on the bishops by the contingencies of history, but it also seems Christ-like in its ability to listen to and to love the other person. Naturally, there are many for whom this form of authority is an evasion of leadership and a betrayal of the gospel. But perhaps this is based on a fear of opening themselves up to the deep listening that comes with Christ-like vulnerability. It is Christ who remains the centre of this new catholic vision – and that is the same Christ who refused to lord it over others; the same Christ who listens to others; and the same Christ who risked everything for the sake of others.

Bibliography

Chapman, Mark D., 'Where is it all going? A plea for humility?' in Kenneth Stevenson (ed.), *A Fallible Church*, London: DLT, 2008, pp. 122–41

Chapman, Mark D., *Doing God: Religion and Public Policy in Brown's Britain*, London: DLT, 2008

Chapman, Mark D. (ed.), *The Anglican Covenant*, London: Mowbray, 2007

Chapman, Mark D., *Anglicanism: A Very Short Introduction*, Oxford: Oxford University Press, 2006

Dancer, Anthony (ed.), *William Stringfellow in Anglo-American Perspective*, Aldershot: Ashgate, 2005

Doll, Peter, *Revolution, Religion and National Identity*, Madison: Farleigh Dickinson, 2000

Jacob, W. M., *The Making of the Anglican Church Worldwide*, London: SPCK, 1997

Jewel, John, in John Ayre (ed.), *The Works of Bishop John Jewel*, 4 vols, Cambridge: Cambridge University Press for the Parker Society, 1845–50, vols. 1 and 3

Sachs, William L., *The Transformation of Anglicanism*, Cambridge: Cambridge University Press, 1993

Stephenson, Alan M. G., *Anglicanism and the Lambeth Conferences*, London: SPCK, 1978

Stephenson, Alan M. G., *The First Lambeth Conference: 1867*, London: SPCK, 1967

Stringfellow, William, *Count It All Joy: Reflections on Faith, Doubt, and Temptation*, Grand Rapids: Eerdmans, 1967

Strong, Rowan, *Anglicanism and the British Empire, c. 1700–1850*, Oxford: Oxford University Press, 2007

Sykes, Norman, *Church and State: Report of the Archbishop's Commission on the Relations Between Church and State*, London: Church Assembly, 1936

Williams, Rowan, February 2008, 'Civil and Religious Law in England: A Religious Perspective' in *Ecclesiastical Law Journal* 10, pp. 262–82

Williams, Rowan, 'Being Biblical Persons' in Anthony Dancer (ed.), *William Stringfellow*, Ashgate, 2005, pp. 184–7

Williams, Rowan, *On Christian Theology*, Oxford: Blackwell, 2000

Notes

1 http://www.aco.org/vault/Reflections%20document.pdf

2 All the archbishop's speeches and addresses at Lambeth can be found at: http://www.lambethconference.org/index.cfm

3 1559 Act of Supremacy

4 On the covenant, see *The Anglican Covenant* (Chapman: 2007)

5 Peter Akinola, address at the opening of Gafcon, 22 June 2008 at: http://www.gafcon.org/index.php?option=com_content&task=view&id=57&Itemid=29

6 See my *Doing God: Religion and Public Policy in Brown's Britain* (Chapman: 2008b), chs 5 and 6.

7 These included his controversial lecture at the Royal Courts of Justice in February 2008, 'Civil and Religious Law in England: A Religious Perspective' in *Ecclesiastical Law Journal* 10, pp. 262–82. This includes answers to questions.

8 'A higher responsibility': Interview with Bishop Paul Richardson for the *Church of England Newspaper*, 8 May 2008 at: http://www.archbishopofcanterbury.org/1835

9 Transcript from Press Conference, 3 August 2008, chaired by Phillip Aspinall, Archbishop of Brisbane, with the Archbishop of Canterbury Rowan Williams.

THE BISHOP AND ANGLICAN IDENTITY

Signposts for Episcopal Character

Stephen Pickard

Introduction: Anglican identity

The recent statement *The Anglican Way: Signposts on a Common Journey* begins with a short depiction of Anglican identity:

> The Anglican Way is a particular expression of the Christian Way of being the One, Holy, Catholic and Apostolic Church of Jesus Christ. It is formed by and rooted in Scripture, shaped by its worship of the living God, ordered for communion, and directed in faithfulness to God's mission in the world. In diverse global situations Anglican life and ministry witnesses to the incarnate, crucified and risen Lord, and is empowered by the Holy Spirit. Together with all Christians, Anglicans hope, pray and work for the coming of the reign of God.[1]

There are four key elements in the above statement: formed by Scripture; shaped by worship; ordered for communion; and directed to God's mission in the world.[2] How might a bishop in the Anglican tradition serve such a vision of the Church? How important for the office and work of a bishop are the four elements? This chapter will explore these two questions and relate them to the promises made by a bishop at consecration. In doing so I hope to show that the four elements identified as belonging to the Anglican Way also belong to the marks of the episcopate and that as a result Episcopal character and Anglican identity are closely related to each other like two sides of the same coin. As such Scripture, worship, communion and mission lie at the heart of the Episcopal calling and are embedded in the promises made by a bishop at consecration.

Signposts for Episcopal character

Some important links between Anglican identity and Episcopal character can be found in *The Anglican Way: The Significance of the Episcopal Office for the Communion of the Church*.[3] The ten theses articulated in this document do not pretend to offer an exhaustive account of the theology of the episcopate. However, they do offer an important theological reflection on the nature and calling of a bishop in the Anglican tradition. The document argues that fundamental to a bishop's life is the role of drawing together the body of Christ and pointing it to the risen Christ. As a witness to the resurrection the bishop leads the community of faith deeper into the gospel. The bishop is thus called to connect people together following the lead and example of Jesus. An appeal is made to the African word, *ubuntu*, which means connectivity. A bishop's connecting role stretches between creation and salvation; people are reconnected to each other, to the earth and to God. In this way a bishop as *community connection person* is tied up with the salvation of all things. This of course is a big claim. Yet even secular historians note that the office of bishop was a truly novel development in early Christianity; it did not have any substantial antecedents (Fox: 1991, ch. 10). The advent of the gospel brought about a new state of affairs and the office and work of a bishop emerged as a way of pointing to this new way of living together under God.

At the end of the document a question is posed as to whether it might be possible to develop the notion of an Episcopal character following on from the idea of a baptismal character. The present chapter is concerned to understand how the office of bishop can be a signpost to the resurrection for the community. Perhaps the way a bishop does this and embodies this for the community and wider society constitutes the Episcopal calling and character. I pursue this line of inquiry by relating the four elements of the Anglican Way identified above to the office of a bishop and Episcopal vows.

Formed by Scripture

At the consecration of a bishop, prior to the making of promises, there appears an exhortation (or 'examination'; 'declaration') outlining the responsibilities and challenges relating to the office of bishop.[4] An unmistakable common thread appearing in the many Ordinals of the Communion concerns the priority of witness to Christ's resurrection and the faithful 'proclamation', 'exposition', 'protection' and 'interpretation' of the gospel. This vital link between bishop and gospel gives force to the proposal many years ago by the former Archbishop of Canterbury and scholar, Michael Ramsey. For Ramsey the episcopate, belonging as it did to the catholic structure of the Church, was 'an utterance of the gospel' and no less (Ramsey: 1936, pp. 54, 208). The episcopate – and for that matter the other orders – were not separate from the reality of the Church but rather organically related to it. The Episcopal office as an utterance of the gospel corresponded, in Ramsey's theology, with 'the utterance of God's redemptive love' (Ramsey: 1936, p. 67).

Familiarity with the promises made by a bishop at consecration will show how important the sacred Scriptures are for the office of a bishop in the Anglican Church. Promises made in relation to the Holy Scriptures are the first promises made by bishops. The Scriptures are the first 'port of call' for a bishop for the very good reason that they 'contain' and 'reveal' everything necessary for eternal salvation through faith in Jesus Christ. Thus in the *Book of Common Prayer* of the Episcopal Church, even prior to the

Examination, the bishop-elect solemnly declares 'the Holy Scriptures of the Old and New Testament to be the Word of God, and to contain all things necessary to salvation' (EC 513). Anglican Ordinals are clear and uncompromising: a bishop's life is marked by the reading, diligent study and teaching of Scripture, and the interpretation of the gospel. Such engagement is to equip, enlighten, stir up and encourage the people of God. In the process faith is deepened, and a bishop is made fit 'to bear witness to the truth of the gospel' (CoE 62). A corollary of this calling is the expectation that the bishop will defend and guard the faith; 'refuting error' (CoE 62). The bishop is thus called to 'correct and set aside teaching contrary to the mind of Christ' (AustPB 803). A Scripture-formed Episcopal office calls people 'to maturity, to the measure of the full stature of Christ . . .' to 'the truth as it is in Jesus' (Eph. 4.13b, 21).

This may seem simple enough though clearly it doesn't just happen. A Scripture-formed Episcopal ministry requires an investment of time, energy and disciplined prayer (as the Ordinals repeatedly make clear). In the busy life of a modern bishop the care of the Church can be so consuming that the study and meditation upon Scripture is short-changed.[5] The Anglican emphasis on Morning and Evening Prayer with the use of the Lectionary is a time-honoured way by which Anglicans might continually 'hear, read, learn, mark and inwardly digest' the Holy Scriptures. This allusion to a well-known prayer used by Anglicans since the Reformation[6] gives credence to the old adage that 'we become what we eat'. A bishop's food for the Episcopal pilgrimage is first of all the Scriptures. This also requires familiarity with the rich inheritance of Scripture interpretation in the ecumenical creeds of the early Church, *The Book of Common Prayer*, and Anglican formularies such as the Articles of Religion, Catechisms and the Lambeth Quadrilateral.

It is also the case that our engagement with Scripture does not occur in a vacuum. We read the Bible in one hand and the newspaper in the other. But of course the matter goes deeper than that. Our different cultures and contexts shape the way we hear and interpret the Holy Scriptures. The Apostle Paul was forever connecting Scripture with new contexts in his missionary travels and in this he was simply following in the footsteps of Jesus who constantly wrestled with Scripture in his teaching and preaching ministry. New situations required new responses and fresh interpretations. A Scripture-formed bishop is a person called to wrestle like Jacob with the Angel (Gen. 32.24–31) to discern the truth of God and bear witness to it. Scripture in this sense is more than a 'tool kit' of truth. It is more truly the living voice of God that has to be listened for and prayed with. Promises to continue to study and deepen faith give weight to the teaching office of the episcopate and the bishop's calling as a pastor theologian of the Church. Liturgically this is signified by the giving of a Bible and the wearing of an Episcopal ring with a stone of amethyst; a symbol of one who seeks wisdom.

Shaped by worship

A bishop is regularly identified as the Church's 'chief pastor' or 'shepherd' charged with the responsibility of gathering God's people (CoE 55). As 'principal ministers of word and sacrament' (CoE 61) or 'chief celebrant' (EC 522) it is the responsibility of bishops to 'preside at the Lord's table' (CoE 61), 'feed and tend the flock' (AustPB 805) and in this way 'serve the royal priesthood' (CoE 55). This points to a sacramental understanding of the Episcopal office; an understanding which has been confirmed in multiple bilateral conversations between Anglican and other churches.[7]

The link between Episcopal office and worship, particularly focused in the eucharistic celebration, is highly significant for Anglicans because it points to the deep connection between worship, ecclesial identity and the role of the bishop in that weave. Worship of the Holy God has primary place in the life of the body of Christ. In an age that is obsessed with production, consumption, and progress through technology and science the activity and orientation of life towards the holiness of God strikes many as odd if not wasteful of energy. Yet a haunting question lies over so much human activity and ways in the world: wherein lies its well-being? The answer given by millennia of Christian witness locates the 'fullest intensity of well-being' in relation to the holiness of God who is creator, redeemer and sustainer of all things (Hardy: 2001, p. 8). Worship concentrates and exemplifies this deepest, richest and most intense holiness of God. Thus we might say that 'Facing the holiness of God, and performing it within social life, is the special provenance of worship' (Hardy: 2001, p. 19). This suggests that worship is not primarily about ascending to God but rather the manner in which human beings 'are held, and moved forward, by the very holiness of God' (Hardy: 2001, p. 20). We are profoundly formed and freed by the 'energizing attraction of the holiness of God' (Hardy: 2001, p. 20). There is much more that needs to be said here but enough has been said to show why worship is so fundamental to our way of being in the world and how significant is the responsibility of those charged to gather, teach, lead, and preside in the divine liturgy. The mode of worship concentrates what is ordinarily spread out; the maximal openness to God in worship exemplifies and enacts what makes for human well-being in extended time and space.

On this account worship is central to questions of identity, purpose and action in the world. That is reason enough for the heavy investment by Anglicans in liturgical life, cultivation of ways sacramental and prayer life, listening to Scripture using lectionary and preaching. Worship might be understood as the whole of life in a little: an intensity of God's gift of truth and holiness to complement the extensity of the same in the world (Hardy: 2001, p. 111). In worship 'the spread-out-ness of life *in situ* is returned in thanks and the compassionate gift of truth and holiness is most fully realized' (Hardy: 2001, p. 112).

Within the Anglican polity and high view of worship sketched above it is the bishop who presides at the local celebration of word and sacrament; who symbolically embodies the Church's offering to God in worship. It is a representative ministry, a relational office in so far as the whole people of God are gathered with the bishop and participate in worship. And in the complexities of ecclesial life this representative ministry is also simultaneously a shared ministry.

It is also entirely appropriate that at an Episcopal consecration a bishop promises to follow the way of worship embodied in *The Book of Common Prayer* (1662) and/or its authorized derivatives. This reflects a long-held though not uncontested view that Anglican identity is deeply formed by its liturgical provisions. As one commentator said some years ago: for Anglicans, 'the liturgy of the Church creates the power base for the Christian community as a whole' (Sykes: 1978, p. 96). A corollary of this is that a bishop is a 'guardian of the faith and sacraments' (CoE 67).

Anglican polity is designed with theological intent, i.e., in order to facilitate the whole people of God 'learning wisdom' (Hardy: 2001, p. 112). The office of the bishop embodies that wisdom tradition in representative ways; perhaps none more so than in being chief pastor and celebrant at those acts of worship which concentrate the community's thanks and praise.

Ordered for communion

It is tempting to move directly from worship to mission as its natural complement. This also makes sense when we think of worship in terms of the intensive engagement compared to Christian life in its extensive or spread-out form. They are really two sides of the same coin. However, the way we order our worship and the way in which we exercise our discipleship in the world are deeply related and thoroughly ecclesial in character. Anglicans are a people knit together through worship and witness. The former doesn't happen in a haphazard manner and nor does our witness in the world occur entirely on an ad hoc basis. The holiness and truth of God moves us forward in worship and in mission in the world. To be ordered according to God's holy way of truth is the intent underlying Anglican liturgical life and mission. For this reason Anglicans give particular attention to the fact that our life in both intensive and extensive modes is ordered in a way that recognizes God's holiness and truth as the deepest reality of the world. Thus Anglicans can rightly speak of being a people ordered for communion: with God, one another and the world for which Christ died and rose.

If the bishop is the chief pastor and celebrant in our ordered worship – following the charismata of the Spirit – then we would anticipate that a bishop, within an Anglican polity, would have chief responsibility for ordered witness and mission. How then might a bishop contribute to the communion of the Church? What then makes for communion or *koinonia*?

Earlier we noted *The Anglican Way: The Significance of the Episcopal Office for the Communion of the Church*. This document articulated ten theses identifying how the office of the episcopate contributed to the *koinonia* of the Church. We noted that the bishop was a *community connection person*, which included a reference to God, others and the world. This is signalled at consecration. For example an important promise made at consecration relates to discipline (EC 518; AustPB 803), correction, maintenance and promotion of 'quietness, peace and love', reconciliation (CoE 62); building the body of Christ in unity, truth and love (Aust PB 803–4); and the aim to 'strive for the visible unity of Christ's Church' (CoE 62). According to the terms of the various declarations a bishop is likewise a person under the discipline and authority of the Church (CoE 63; EC 513; AustPB 800–1).

The consecration promises also include a common reference to the bishop sharing the 'government of the Church' (EC 518) with presbyters; being the one to 'guide and strengthen deacons'; and working 'with your fellow servants in the gospel' (CoE 62), 'encouraging those committed to [the bishop's] care to fulfill their ministry' (AustPB 804) as they build up the life of the Church. Episcopal identity in terms of communion revolves around the affirmation, coordination and development of the diverse callings of the whole people of God. However, it is clear from the Ordinal that a bishop serves the communion of the Church as he/she is asked to fashion their own life and that of their household in the way of Christ (CoE 62); through attention to his/her own life of prayer and hospitality (CoE 62); being a 'wholesome example for the entire flock of Christ' (EC 517); 'living modestly, in justice and godliness' (AustPB 63).

Koinonia is the business of the episcopate because it is the business of the gospel. Thus we are not surprised at the Episcopal weighting of the so-called Four Instruments of Communion (Archbishop of Canterbury; Lambeth Conference; Anglican Consultative Council and Primates' Meeting). These formal instruments offer cohesion to global Anglicanism, limit the centralization of authority and rely on bonds of affection for effective functioning. At this point Anglican identity and Episcopal character mesh. This is symbolized in the giving of the pastoral staff as sign of being a shepherd with oversight for the well-being of the flock.

Directed by God's mission

Anglican identity is incomplete without its strong missional emphasis. In this sense our Church is at heart an Apostolic Church. Theologically it is founded upon the incarnation of the eternal Word, enfleshed and dwelling among us, ministering and suffering; dying and being raised and empowering a new discipleship; an apostolic movement. The sentness (*apostolos*) of the Church is fundamental to Anglican identity. This claim is given real force by the fact that the Anglican Church has spread in a short period of time from being the Church of England to a Communion of over 80 million people in over 160 countries around the globe.

A bishop is an apostolic person at heart. The first task of the bishop is to bear witness to the resurrection of Christ. This is the primary apostolic calling. A bishop 'is called to be one with the apostles in proclaiming Christ's resurrection' (EC 517). The prayer at the laying on of hands calls upon the Lord to 'fill this your servant with the grace and power which you gave to your apostles' (CoE 67). In a nuanced manner the Ordinals suggest a close bond between the original apostolic impulse in the gospel and the order of bishops in the Anglican Church. The Ordinals often draw upon the tradition of prayer before the calling of the apostles (AustPB 802) and the appointment of Matthias (AustPB 805; EC 514). Bishops are 'guardians of the faith (CoE 55) and teachers of the apostles' (CoE 61) and the prayer is for an 'increase in the Church' (CoE 67). The apostolic calling and identity of an Anglican bishop is clear from the Ordinal.

What does being sent in mission like the apostles entail? It means 'proclaiming the gospel to all' 'to the ends of the earth' (EC 66); 'in all the world' (CoE 63); being 'heard in every place' (CoE 62) and being an encourager of others 'to make disciples of all nations'; extending compassion and mercy 'to the poor and stranger' and defending those 'who have no helper' (AustPB 803–4; EC 518) or 'have no other to speak for them' (CoE 62). This is pre-eminently a ministry imitating Jesus Christ who is our pattern.[8]

Living by promise: Ecclesial and Episcopal identity

The above discussion of the bishop and Anglican identity has shown how the Episcopal vows of a bishop relate to four critical aspects of Anglican identity. These four elements – Scripture, worship, communion and mission – may not be unique to Anglicanism but they are certainly characteristic of what it means to be of the Anglican Communion. These four elements are not exhaustive; however, they do offer reliable signposts for those seeking to follow the Christian way today. And as we have observed at the outset of our discussion these four elements are central features of a broad depiction of Anglicanism. However, as we are well aware identity is never a steady-state affair but is a constantly evolving and dynamic matter. The course of Anglican history and its remarkable expansion has increased the richness, diversity and power of Anglicanism.

Yet throughout the evolution of Anglicanism it is possible to discern some enduring elements and preoccupations that give a certain constancy through change. These 'red threads' running through the complex Anglican weave have been identified in terms of the four elements of Scripture, worship, communion and mission. In more recent times the mission element has assumed greater significance. However, that has been undergirded theologically by a Scripture-formed faith, a worship-shaped life and an ordered approach to life in communion. The interplay of the four elements is critical for a healthy, outward-directed and invitational approach to being the body of Christ in the world.

What is quite remarkable is that the revised Ordinal of 1550 for the consecration of bishops, as it become grafted into the *Book of Common Prayer*, 1662, has a strong correlation with the enduring elements of Anglican identity as noted above. Although there have been changes to the form and content of the ordination promises made by a bishop, nonetheless it is possible to discern the continuing importance of the four elements of Anglicanism embedded in Episcopal vows. This ought not to be surprising but it begs a question. To what extent has the character and identity of Anglicanism been shaped by its Episcopal polity and to what extent has the latter simply reflected the Anglican ideal? It may be sufficient in this essay simply to state the question and suggest that the course of Anglican history shows a constant interweaving of the Episcopal character of its life and its identity as a particular expression of the Universal Church of Jesus Christ. The Anglican Church cannot be without its bishops and its bishops are profoundly shaped and ordered by their being of this particular Communion.

I have drawn attention to the significance of the promises made at consecration as the window into the relationship between the bishop and Anglican identity. The form and content of such Episcopal promises varies throughout the Communion in certain respects and this essay is not the place to rehearse this. However I am reasonably confident that the Ordinals across the Communion show a remarkable constancy in their focus on the four elements of Anglicanism: Scripture, worship, communion and mission. This suggests that amidst the many controversies that embroil the Communion at this time in its life, amidst the many claims and counter-claims about what constitutes Anglican identity and orthodoxy, the vows taken by a bishop at consecration offer an important guide and pattern for the life of a bishop and the whole Church. This is perhaps exactly as it should be because it reminds us and recalls us back to the centrality of promise for the standing or the falling of the Church. As a Communion we live by promise. In the first instance a bishop is a true bishop of the people in so far as that person lives in and from their Episcopal promises. A renewed focus on the vows offers a far richer framework in which to make assessments about the quality and capabilities of those called to the office of the episcopate. In a deeper sense the Church lives by its baptismal promises. The life of discipleship is a life lived in and under and from promises.

We are only too well aware of the frailty of human life, the darkness of the human heart and the inevitable 'break at the heart of every promise' that haunts our life, church and society.[9] We have to learn over and over again that we are made and maintained as a Communion and as persons by being bonded in worship and witness to the God of promise whose constancy and faithfulness is eternal. Our identity is tied up with an understanding of ourselves as worshipping selves (Ford: 1999, p. 97); as a Communion given over to the worship of the living God, as a people called to declare the wonderful deeds of the One Jesus Christ who called us out of darkness into the wonderful light of the Lord (1 Pet. 2.9). The vows a bishop makes are truly a window for the Church into the deepest secrets of its life and the deepest secrets about how its life is constantly renewed and its identity is shaped and energized by the God and Father of our Lord Jesus Christ.

Bibliography

Anglican Church of Australia, *A Prayer Book for Australia*, Musgrave, Victoria: Broughton Books, 1995

Church of England, *Common Worship: Ordination Services Study Edition*, London: Church House Publishing, 2007

Episcopal Church, *The Book of Common Prayer*, New York: Seabury Press, 1979

Ford, David, *Self and Salvation: Being Transformed*, Cambridge: Cambridge University Press, 1999

Fox, Robin Lane, *Pagans and Christians*, New York: Viking Press, 1991

Hardy, Daniel W., *Finding the Church: The Dynamic Truth of Anglicanism*, London: SCM Press, 2001

Pickard, Stephen, 'The Travail of the Episcopate: Management and the Diocese in an Age of Mission' in B. Kaye, S. Macneil and H. Thomson (eds), *Wonderfully and Confessedly Strange: Australian Essays in Anglican Ecclesiology*, Adelaide: ATF Press, 2006, pp. 127–55

Ramsey, Arthur Michael, *The Gospel and the Catholic Church*, London: Longmans, Green and Co., 1936

Ricoeur, Paul, *Oneself as Another*, trans. Kathleen Blamey, Chicago: University of Chicago Press, 1992

Signposts Series, no. 1, *The Anglican Way: Signposts on a Common Journey*, London: Anglican Communion Office, 2008

Sykes, Stephen, *The Integrity of Anglicanism*, London: Mowbray, 1978

Wilberforce, Robert, *The Doctrine of the Incarnation of our Lord Jesus Christ in relation to Mankind and to the Church*, Philadelphia: 1849

Notes

1 See the Anglican Communion website: www.anglicancommunion.org/ministry/theological/signposts/

2 For an extended reflection on the four key elements of the Anglican Way see the Signposts Series, 2008, and at the Anglican Communion website: www.anglicancommunion.org/ministry/theological/signposts/

3 See the appendix to the recent Inter-Anglican Theological and Doctrinal Commission's report, *Communion, Conflict and Hope*, London: Anglican Communion Office, 2008, pp. 56–67. Also at the Anglican Communion website: www.anglicancommunion.org/ministry/theological/iatdc/docs/communion

4 For the purposes of this brief essay I have used three Ordinals: Episcopal Church, 1979, *The Book of Common Prayer*, pp. 512–24 (hereafter EC); Church of England, 2007, *Common Worship: Ordination Services Study Edition*, pp. 54–76 (hereafter CoE); Anglican Church of Australia, 1995, *A Prayer Book for Australia*, pp. 799–809 (hereafter AustPB).

5 For a discussion of the tensions between diocesan responsibilities, management mission and the claims of the Episcopal vows see Pickard: 2006.

6 The prayer used to be the Collect for the Second Sunday in Advent (often called Bible Sunday) though it has been shifted in many Anglican Churches a few weeks earlier. The full text is worth quoting:

Blessed Lord,
You have caused all holy Scriptures to be written

for our learning:
grant that we may so hear them,
read, mark, learn and inwardly digest them,
that, by patience and comfort of your holy word,
we may embrace and ever hold fast
the blessed hope of everlasting life,
which you have given us in our Saviour Jesus Christ. Amen.

7 For further details see the ecumenical documents on the Anglican Communion website: www.anglicancommunion.org/ministry/ecumenical/commissions/iascer

8 It was the nineteenth-century Anglican theologian, Robert Wilberforce, who developed the idea of 'Christ the pattern man' and in so doing offered a rich account of the humanity of Christ. See Wilberforce: 1849.

9 Paul Ricoeur refers to the 'break at the heart of every promise' as a feature of our life as humans (1992).

2

CELEBRATING COMMON GROUND

The Bishop and Anglican Identity

Clive Handford

Throughout Anglican history, the existence of the episcopate has been a constant characteristic. Six of the 38 Anglican churches have the term 'Episcopal' in their title. In ecumenical conversations, the episcopate has always been an element held as a requirement for union.

From the end of the first century there have been bishops. At the English Reformation, the supremacy of the Pope was replaced by that of the King: Henry VIII. Bishops remained, concerned to ensure the continued succession with their predecessors. The Sovereign, the 'Godly Prince', did not seek to change that. The bishops were the King's ministers for the spiritual care and government of the nation. The Ordinal of Edward VI stated that 'it is evident . . . that from the Apostles' time there have been these Orders of Ministers in Christ's Church: Bishops, Priests and Deacons'. While subsequent research into the origins of the Church's ministry may have somewhat tempered the confidence of that assertion, its significance in its historical context is clear. Any objection of the English Reformers to episcopacy was not to bishops as such but to the way they often exercised their ministry. The prelatical ways to which the reformers objected were not, of course, entirely overcome. Bishops were the King's officers and so a certain continuing element of worldly power was not altogether surprising.

After the break with Rome and before 1662, most Anglicans seemed to accept the Reformed Churches of Europe as valid churches even though without bishops. There are recorded instances of ministers from these churches being accepted into the ministry of the Church of England without being required to undergo Episcopal ordination. This changed from 1662 when the Act of Uniformity required that all Anglican clergy should be episcopally ordained.

After 1688, nine bishops and several hundred priests refused to make the Oath of Allegiance to the new sovereign. They were deprived of their sees and benefices and new bishops consecrated in their place. Several of those deprived secretly consecrated successors so as to preserve what they considered a true Episcopal succession. This focused the question as to whether succession through the episcopate is integral to the life of the Church and unbreakable by outside authority, notably the state. What might be termed this 'High Church' view was, at least in part, a reaction against the increasingly secular and political understanding of the episcopate which developed in the eighteenth century. It was picked up strongly by the Oxford Movement in the years following 1833.

It was in this atmosphere that there appeared in 1870 in the United States of America a publication entitled *The Church Idea*. The work of William Reed Huntington, a New York rector, it contained what has come to be known as the Chicago–Lambeth Quadrilateral. Adopted by the House of Bishops of PECUSA in Chicago in 1886 and by the Lambeth Conference of 1888 it is quoted to this day as a fundamental Anglican formula and the basis on which unity with other churches will be pursued. The fourth of its four points affirms 'The Historic Episcopate, locally adapted in the methods of its administration to the varying needs of the nations and peoples called of God into the Unity of His Church'. Seen in conjunction with the preceding three points, the Holy Scriptures, the Creeds and the Sacraments, the episcopate has a clear role in the embodiment of the catholicity, apostolicity and unity of the Church.

However, as Dr Vincent, Assistant Bishop of Southern Ohio, sought to make clear during the debates that took place in the 1880s, the phrase 'the historic episcopate' 'was deliberately chosen as declaring not a doctrine but a fact and as being general enough to include all variants'. The aim was to fashion as broad a doctrine of episcopacy as possible within the limitations imposed by the realities of church history while affirming the importance of tradition in history. The Report of the Joint Commission on Approaches to Unity to the American General Convention of 1949 said that episcopacy is 'a fact accompanied by its historical meaning'.

The Lambeth Conference of 1920 was firm that Anglicans did not seek to deny 'the spiritual reality of the ministries of the communions which do not possess the episcopate'. But it affirmed that the episcopate is 'the best instrument for maintaining the unity of the Church'. The 1958 Conference, while again not seeking to 'unchurch' other communions, affirmed more strongly the belief 'that a ministry acknowledged by every part of the Church can only be attained through the historic episcopate'.

There have been differing views about the nature and theology of episcopacy and variation in the way it has been exercised and perceived in society at large. Notwithstanding this, the role of the historic episcopate has remained an integral part of Anglican identity and self-understanding.

This is a very cursory acknowledgement of history in the development of the Anglican understanding of episcopacy. From it we must now turn to examine some of the formulae and structures of the Anglican Communion which embody the understanding of episcopacy today.

In a paper prepared for the Lambeth Conference of 2008 by the International Standing Commission on Ecumenical Relations (IASCER) entitled 'The Ministry of Bishops in Ecumenical Perspective', the writers quote from the Porvoo Agreement: 'Oversight of the Church and its mission is the particular responsibility of the bishop. The bishop's office is one of service and communication within the community of believers and, together with the whole community, to the world. Bishops preach the word, preside at the sacraments, and administer discipline in such a way as to be representative pastoral ministers of oversight of the area to which they are called. They serve the apostolicity, catholicity and unity of the Church's teaching, worship and sacramental life. They have responsibility for leadership in the Church's mission.' In a reference to the Cyprus Agreed Statement of the Anglican–Orthodox Theological Dialogue, IASCER notes:

> As dioceses grew in size, presbyters in addition to bishops became the normal eucharistic ministers. In due course, the bishop's eucharistic role became overshadowed by administrative and judicial functions. Even his ministry as the teacher of the Church came to be separated from his preaching ministry. This weakened the bishop's primary role as president of the Eucharist. There was thus a fading of the earlier local, eschatological and eucharistic self-understanding of the Church. What is important in this vision for Anglicans is not that the bishop always presides at the Eucharist in the local parish, but that theologically the bishop is understood to be the chief pastor, teacher, preacher and president of the Eucharist for the diocese. It is primarily in this way that the bishop is the sign of *koinonia* at all levels of the Church's life.

The Lambeth Conference of 1988 outlined a number of elements that are involved in the exercise of Episcopal ministry. The bishop is:

1. a symbol of the Unity of the Church in its mission;
2. a teacher and defender of the faith;
3. pastor of the pastors and of the laity;
4. an enabler in the preaching of the Word, and in the administration of the Sacraments;
5. a leader in mission and an initiator of outreach to the world surrounding the community of the faithful;
6. a shepherd who nurtures and cares for the flock of God;

45

7. a physician to whom are brought the wounds of society;
8. a voice of conscience within the society in which the local Church is placed;
9. a prophet who proclaims the justice of God in the context of the Gospel of loving redemption;
10. a head of the family in its wholeness, its misery and its joy. The bishop is the family's centre of life and love.

The Inter-Anglican Theological and Doctrinal Commission was asked by the Archbishop of Canterbury to produce a paper to guide and stimulate the thinking of the bishops at the 2008 Lambeth Conference. Under the title *The Anglican Way: The Significance of the Episcopal Office for the Communion of the Church*, the Commission advanced ten theses, with a commentary on each. These theses (without the commentary) are:

Thesis One: The bishop serves the *koinonia* of the gospel into which the baptized are incorporated by God the Holy Spirit.
Thesis Two: The bishop's evangelical office of proclamation and witness is a fundamental means by which those who hear the call of God become one in Christ.
Thesis Three: The bishop is a teacher and defender of the apostolic faith that binds believers in one body.
Thesis Four: The bishop has oversight (*episcope*) of the household of God for the good order of the Church.
Thesis Five: The bishop is called to co-ordinate the gifts of the people of God for the building up of the faithful for the furtherance of God's mission.
Thesis Six: The bishop serves the *koinonia* of the gospel through care, encouragement and discipline of the pastors of the Church.
Thesis Seven: The bishop serves the *koinonia* of the gospel through a ministry of mediation to recall the broken and conflicted body of Christ to its reconciled life in him.
Thesis Eight: The catholicity of the Episcopal office connects the baptized across boundaries of culture, class, gender, race and lands, and enables the Church to realize its oneness in Christ.

Thesis Nine: The bishop serves the collegial life of the Church through the nurture of strong bonds with bishops of the Anglican Communion and those who share *episcope* in other Christian churches.

Thesis Ten: A diocesan bishop is given responsibility for *episcope* in the particular place where the bishop is principal pastor.

To these two outlines of the nature and understanding of the bishop's ministry may be added the 'Reflections of the Bishops at the Lambeth Conference 2008':

> As bishops, we are committed to the life of the Church, to the wider communities in which we minister and to civil society. We recognize that it is our calling to be bridge-builders, reconcilers and symbols of unity, representing the local to the universal and the universal to the local, taking our place within the world-wide college of bishops across the Communion within the one Church of Christ.

The unity of the Anglican Communion has been seriously impaired in the last five years by the consecration as bishop of a person living in a partnered homosexual relationship, by public rites of blessing of same-sex unions, and by the intervention in the North American Churches of bishops and primates from other provinces. One of the responses to this is the proposal of an Anglican Covenant. The second draft, known as the St Andrew's Draft, was commended to the churches of the Communion in March 2008 and discussed by the bishops at the Lambeth Conference. The idea of a covenant has not found universal acceptance but at the Lambeth Conference, the first Communion-wide testing of the concept, there emerged 'a willingness to continue exploring a Covenant together'. One of the articles of the draft Covenant affirms

> the central role of bishops as guardians and teachers of faith, leaders in mission, and as a visible sign of unity, representing the universal Church to the local, and the local church to the universal. This ministry is exercised personally, collegially

and within and for the Eucharistic community. We receive and maintain the historic threefold ministry of bishops, priests and deacons, ordained for service in the Church of God, as they call all the baptized into the mission of Christ.

There have developed over the years four bodies that have come to be known as the 'Instruments of Communion'. They serve the articulation of the common life of the Communion and so are potentially major indicators of Anglican identity. Three of the four are entirely Episcopal in composition and bishops have an important role in the fourth.

The Archbishop of Canterbury is in some ways the primary symbol of the Anglican Communion. One of the essentials of Anglican membership is being 'in communion with the See of Canterbury'. Canterbury Cathedral is seen as the Mother Church of the Communion. The writer remembers at the Lambeth Conference of 1998 seeing members moved to tears when they saw the cathedral for the first time.

The Archbishop of Canterbury is described as having an 'extraordinary ministry of *episcope*, support and reconciliation'. The *Windsor Report* used the description: 'the central focus of unity and mission within the Communion [with authority] to speak directly to any provincial situation on behalf of the Communion where this is deemed advisable'.

In many quarters, in the wider Church and the wider world, the Archbishop of Canterbury is seen as *the* symbol of the Anglican Communion, the embodiment of Anglican identity, and often as the authority figure to whom all relate. On a number of occasions, as a bishop and a primate, he was referred to in conversation as 'my boss'! This represents a popular misconception of the Anglican reality and the way the Communion works. The archbishop is 'first among equals', accorded a primacy of honour but without jurisdiction outside his own province. There have been proposals at various times recently to enhance the role, sometimes by attempting to make more formal the 'trouble-shooting' element in the archbishop's ministry in the Communion as a whole. While there has been no clear answering of such proposals, fears of an

'Anglican Papacy' usually lurk quite close to the surface. In some quarters, resistance to any enhanced role seems to come from uneasiness about the way in which the Archbishop of Canterbury is appointed. As a bishop of the Church of England, the state is involved in his appointment, albeit to a lesser degree in recent years than in times past. In terms of representing Anglican identity, it must be recognized that there are a number of different ways in which bishops are appointed. Seen together in their variety they symbolize something of the breadth of Anglicanism.

The office of the Archbishop of Canterbury can never be totally separated from the person holding the office and, indeed, embodying it. To some extent, the Anglican understanding of a matter is seen in the wider world by the words and actions of the archbishop as the Communion's principal spokesman. One of the features which characterized the Lambeth Conference of 2008 was the great affection in which the present archbishop is held, stemming not least from the way in which he 'owned' the Conference, directing it sensitively, and from his deep personal holiness.

In the history of the Instruments, the next oldest is the Lambeth Conference, first established in 1867 and meeting every ten years. It brings together all the bishops of the Communion. The Conference provides a setting for study, prayer, fellowship and guidance from the bishops for the ongoing life of the Church. Words from the opening of the 'Reflections' document from the 2008 Lambeth Conference capture the experience of all such gatherings:

> Face to face conversations, often exchanging challenging and conflicting points of view, have led to deeper understanding and new insights . . . Written words can never adequately describe the life-changing nature of our time together. We have gained a deeper appreciation of the worldwide Anglican Communion and of our common calling as disciples of Christ.

The Lambeth Conference is not a law-making body. Its resolutions are not binding on the individual provinces of the Communion. However, as the Windsor Continuation Group noted in its submission to the 2008 Conference:

49

While acknowledging that resolutions of one Conference have been reviewed, and decisions changed at a later Conference, nonetheless, like the resolutions taken by councils of bishops in primitive Christianity, they are of sufficient weight that the consciences of many bishops require them to follow or at least try to follow such resolutions. They are taken after due debate and after prayer by the ministers who represent the apostles to their churches.

A painful feature of the recent Lambeth Conference was the absence of more than two hundred bishops. We must return later to consider the significance of this since it clearly has an impact on our Anglican identity and its perception in the wider world.

The Anglican Consultative Council is the only Instrument that comprises more than bishops. It brings together bishops, clergy and laity. Because of this, it is sometimes mistakenly seen as an Anglican Synodical body. In fact, as its name indicates, its role is *consultative*. It seeks to advise, encourage and inform the provinces. From the experience of bishops expressed in the last Lambeth Conference there would seem to be a division of view between some who believe the Council exercises too much authority and those who believe that it should be given more. One of its potential strengths is that it is representative of the whole people of God. The bishops' presence underlines their place in the one body of Christ. They are seen to be part of the one ministry and can never rightly fulfil their calling in isolation from the whole Church in which and for which they were consecrated.

The 'youngest' of the Instruments of Communion, the Primates' Meeting, seems to be the one that arouses most suspicion. Originally called by Archbishop Donald Coggan to enable Communion-wide consultation between Lambeth Conferences, some feel that it is now exercising an unwanted authority. Others believe that in the current situation in the Communion the primates' role is vital. A view emerged in the 'Reflections' from the recent Lambeth Conference that the primates should not exercise collectively any more authority than they have in their own provinces. That is a statement which calls for closer examination. It begs the question of the varying kinds of authority exercised by primates in individual provinces. As with the other Instruments, there often seems a desire to give the body more 'teeth' while at the same time working to extract them.

There is general agreement that more reflection is needed on the working of all the Instruments of Communion, on their relationship to one another and their ability to serve the mission of the Church. In its second presentation to the Lambeth Conference, the Windsor Continuation Group said: 'In considering the future development of the Instruments of Communion it is vital to take account of their ecclesiological significance as well as whether they are fit to respond effectively to the demands of global leadership. There needs to be a process of Communion-wide reflection which leads towards a common understanding.'

It may seem that undue space has been given to consideration of the four Instruments of Communion. This is because the place of the bishop in them is central. A theology of the episcopate, like a bishop's ministry, can never be worked out or lived out in isolation. It is earthed in, and to a degree springs from, the ongoing life both of the Church and of the world. It can never be an abstract idea but, like faith, is *solvitur ambulando*. While not the only way, participation directly or indirectly in the working of the Instruments is the structured way by which the bishop represents the local to the universal and the universal to the local. For this to be realistic, given the actual membership of the different bodies, the collegiality of bishops in Province and Communion is essential. However they may develop, the four Instruments of Communion will remain visible indicators of Anglican identity and of the bishop as a symbol of that identity.

As the bishops at the Lambeth Conference shared their stories and experiences, the significance of the fourth point of the Lambeth Quadrilateral was brought to life: 'The Historic Episcopate, *locally adapted in the methods of its administration* to the varying needs of the nations and peoples called by God into the Unity of His Church' (my italics). Dioceses differ considerably from one another. Some bishops live no more than an hour's travel from the most distant congregation in the diocese. Others may need to travel for several days. Some minister in a variety of permanent buildings while others have few permanent buildings at all. In some cases, the Anglican Church may be the majority Church in a Christian culture. In others the Church may be a minority in a culture dominated by another faith. All this affects the bishop's role and the public perception of it. In places like England, some bishops have a role in the government of their country and are often-quoted public figures. Others may be like tribal leaders or heads of families. A few may be in secular employment. A bishop may have an elaborate supporting administration with clergy and lay people involved. Others will travel very light on structures. There are other variations from place to place but, in and through all, the fundamental role of the bishop as symbol of unity, representative of the Church and leader of mission remains.

Of the descriptions of the nature of episcopacy that have been noted already, two may be singled out for further comment. The bishop is a symbol of unity and a representative person. The understanding of the two overlaps. The breadth of Anglicanism is not always appreciated by those of more 'monochrome' churches, or even within the Communion itself. Recently a comment has been heard from an ecumenical partner which was something like: 'We thought we knew you, now we are not so sure.' The autonomy of the individual Anglican Provinces is not always understood. A sharing with other churches in the historic episcopate does not mean that all function in the same way. Some ecumenical partners have expected a more authoritative (authoritarian?) line to be taken on particular issues. Some would seem to think the Archbishop of Canterbury should adopt the role of a headmaster. That is not the classical Anglican understanding of a bishop, however much in some places and at some times individual bishops may have acted in that way.

A recent statement from a Roman Catholic source said that the Anglican Communion needs to decide whether it is Catholic or Protestant. Such a remark betrays a basic misunderstanding of the nature of Anglicanism which is both Catholic and Reformed. Some bishops, as some other Anglicans, will tend to emphasize one aspect more than the other. However, within the body of the bishops the breadth of Anglicanism is represented. In order that this may be seen, and the insights of different traditions share with one another, the collegiality of bishops both provincially and internationally is essential.

Recent events within the Communion have raised questions about the exercise of provincial autonomy and how it can fit with the so-called 'bonds of affection' which supposedly unite us. It seems that independence is valued more highly than interdependence and bishops can appear more symbols of division that of unity. The Windsor Continuation Group in its Preliminary Observations at the Lambeth Conference, speaking of finding a Way Forward, said: 'If we are to survive as an international family of Churches, then the 2008 *Windsor Report*'s suggestion of a shift of emphasis to "autonomy-in-communion" might yet require a further step to "communion with autonomy and accountability".

As the Lambeth Conference 2008 moved into its second week, the friendship and respect that had been building up in the *indaba* and Bible Study Groups started to show in a growth of mutual understanding. Implications of local actions for the wider family began to be appreciated. Bishops recognized something of the pain being felt by fellow bishops as well as the questions posed by seeking to be true to the gospel in diverse cultures. Persecution and natural disasters became more real to those mercifully spared them through the testimony of those who live with them, sometimes on a daily basis. The complexity of Anglican identity in all its diverse strands became more rooted in the lives of the bishops gathered together. Actions in one place affect another. Perhaps this was typified for many by the words of an African bishop who said: 'Because of our history we were always known as "The State Church"; now we are known as "The Gay Church" – and our children suffer in the playground because of it.' There was a deepening appreciation of how 'when one suffers, all suffer'. It is often by what a bishop says or does, or who is appointed, that Anglicanism and, indeed, Christianity are judged.

A sad feature of the Lambeth Conference this time was the absence of more than two hundred bishops who, out of conscience, did not feel able to accept the Archbishop of Canterbury's invitation. Most of them had been at the Global Anglican Futures Conference (GAFCON) in Jerusalem a few weeks before. 'A house divided' seems increasingly a description of Anglican identity and bishops its spokespersons. Our Lord's warning that 'a house divided against itself will not be able to stand' makes it imperative that urgent efforts are made to build bridges and to engage with others at a deep level across the divides. In large measure, bishops have, one way or another, had a major hand in hardening the divisions. If they are to be true to their calling as symbols of unity they must have a key role in bringing about healing. The bishops who met in Canterbury were re-affirmed in believing the Communion to be precious and that it must be saved. Already there is a degree of impaired communion. For more than one reason, some primates will not share communion with others. Some priests will not receive communion from their bishop or recognize their bishop as a valid minister of the sacraments. Where this impairment exists, is the bishop's symbolizing of unity impaired too?

Current tensions may cause us to re-examine what goes beyond the admissible 'local adaptation' to different cultural contexts envisaged by the Chicago–Lambeth Quadrilateral. Ought not 'local adaptation' be only such as will still allow the episcopate to act collegially, with full interchangeability of ministries and a shared sacramental life under a single episcopate? Some of the developments which have taken place in the Communion recently savour very much of parallel jurisdiction, a situation which, however imperfectly in a few places, the Church since the Council of Nicaea has pledged to avoid.

As the bishops at the Lambeth Conference came to know one another and shared their stories they appreciated again the richness of the Anglican Communion. They were convinced of the importance of it and the need to hold together despite current tensions. There was a real celebrating of common ground. The breadth of traditions, held together in common bonds of affection, is at the heart of Anglican identity. It is the bishop's calling to embody this and express it in word and deed.

3

PROCLAIMING THE
GOOD NEWS

James Tengatenga

Introduction

In many ways this is such an obvious work of the Church that it requires no discussion. However, it is usually the obvious that needs explaining and exploration. Church is about preaching and so is the bishop's task. The bishop, as only one person, cannot do it all and more often than not they do not have the time to do so beyond the confines of confirmation and dedication services. What role if any do they have in this enterprise? The bishop is a leader and it is leading that they are expected to do. What informs that leadership and what resources does the bishop have at hand to do this? How does this role manifest itself in the different contexts in which the bishop exercises their *episcope*? It is not my intention to rehearse the gleanings of the Lambeth *indaba* on this theme. I will, however, use some of the ideas as a springboard from which to launch my reflection.

At the heart of mission is the proclamation of the gospel. Since mission is God's mission it is God's self-disclosure. Proclamation is our part in making that available to all. Proclamation is revelation, that is, making God and God's saving power known through Jesus in the power of the Holy Spirit. I still remember the sermon preached at my ordination to the priesthood some 23 years ago. It was based on John 12.21: 'Sir, we want to see Jesus.' As Jesus Christ himself claims, one who has seen Jesus has seen the Father. Making Christ known is the aim of all proclamation. Jesus sent his disciples out to proclaim the coming of the kingdom of God. These same disciples having become apostles went all over the known world to proclaim this good news. Bishops as the successors of the apostles are called to the same. As such evangelism is not an optional extra for a bishop. It is at the heart of his calling. No wonder one of the Propers for the consecration of Bishops in the Ordinal is Isaiah 61: 'The Spirit of the Lord is upon me. He has sent me to proclaim Good News to the poor . . . and the acceptable year of the Lord.' This was read at my consecration as Bishop and continues to be the theme of my episcopate.

The context (from which, in which and to which the proclamation is done)

The Anglican Communion, through MISSIO, its Mission Commission, has understood this as the mission of God to which all are called. In 1988 the Communion inaugurated the Decade of Evangelism as an expression and a living out of this mission imperative. This activity was not a new innovation. It followed centuries of spreading the gospel all over the world through different mission initiatives. This is what the mission agencies in the Communion are vestiges, expressions and continuations of. It would not be an overstatement to say that the Communion is held together by mission and more specifically the proclamation of the gospel. All our links, partnerships and even our struggles and controversies and divisions have at their centre the proclamation of the Good News. No wonder 'To Proclaim the Good News of the Kingdom of God' is the first of the five marks of mission. This is what this last Lambeth Conference was carrying forward through this theme. Like previous publications (MISAG I and II, *Communion in Mission* and *Anglicans in Mission*) from the

Mission Issues and Strategy Advisory Group, the latest report of the survey of all provincial activities in mission and evangelism, 'Holistic Mission: A profile of mission and evangelism in the Anglican Communion', acknowledges the complexities of the task due to the variety of contexts and the challenges inherent therein. It highlighted ten mission contexts: Other Faiths, Migrants, refugees and displaced people, HIV and AIDS, Response to emergencies, Young people, Reconciliation, Response to decline, Growth, Economic viability and Christian values. These were also given as contexts to be discussed during the Lambeth Conference as bishops shared stories from their contexts. The report also highlighted some challenges to the enterprise, viz., economics, innovations, postmodernity, leadership and leadership training.

Cardinal Ivan Dias, the Prefect of the Congregation for the Evangelization of Peoples in the Roman Catholic Church, in his address to the Conference described the context thus:

The theme of evangelization must be considered in the wider context of the spiritual combat which began in the Garden of Eden with the fall of our first parents, in the wake of fierce hostilities between God and the rebel angels. If this context is ignored in favour of a myopic world-vision, Christ's salvation will be conveniently dismissed as irrelevant.

The spiritual combat, described in the Books of Genesis and Revelation, has continued unabated all down the ages. St Paul described it in very vivid terms: 'We are not contending against flesh and blood, but against principalities and powers, against the world rulers of this present darkness, against the spiritual hosts of wickedness in the heavenly places' (Eph. 6:12). This combat rages fiercely even today, aided and abetted by well-known secret sects, Satanic groups and New Age movements, to mention but a few, and reveals many ugly heads of the hideous anti-God monster: among them are notoriously secularism, which seeks to build a Godless society; spiritual indifference, which is insensitive to transcendental values; and relativism, which is contrary to the permanent tenets of the Gospel. All of these seek to efface any reference to God or to

57

things supernatural, and to supplant it with mundane values and behaviour patterns which purposely ignore the transcendental and the divine. Far from satisfying the deep yearnings of the human heart, they foster a culture of death, be it physical or moral, spiritual or psychological. (Address at Lambeth Conference 2008)

This begs the question of how the bishop responds to this context or contexts. During the retreat at the beginning of the Lambeth Conference Archbishop Rowan Williams described the bishop's role as that of oversight, insight, a linguist and an exemplar. The bishop is a leader in this, whatever his or her churchmanship. Being stuck in one's churchmanship does not always help the enterprise. The bishop should be versatile – thinking and acting outside the box. At the same time he must be willing to let others lead. The task is ecumenical and may lead to strange bedfellows for God's sake! This is the incarnational nature of proclamation. Jesus came and lived among us and proclaimed the Good News of the kingdom of God outside of the box (John 1.14). Proclamation has a kenotic character to it (Philippians 2). Emptying oneself and exposing oneself to all sorts of ridicule and derision is what Jesus the saviour and exemplar did. In him all the Godhead was revealed. Proclamation was commanded by Christ to all who follow him. The Apostle Paul also encouraged others to do the same. To Timothy he also specifically exhorted him to preach 'in season and out of season'. There is a coercion and compulsion in the spreading of the Good News. Once one is committed to Christ one is committed to proclamation. As Christ faced hardships in doing so, he warned his disciples of their share of them. The leading and prompting of the Holy Spirit can be an uncomfortable experience. The prophets of old had that experience. Ezekiel was called to act out his sermons and oracles. Jeremiah even went so far as to complain and accuse God of deceiving him (Jeremiah 20) by giving him the Word to speak to God's people.

This attitude and surrender to the call to evangelize requires a certain kind of vision. St Paul, writing to the Corinthians, talks about it as 'seeing with new eyes': seeing as God sees (2 Cor-inthians 5). Because one sees this way, one recognizes that the world is not what it seems, 'there is a new creation and a new call to the mission of reconciliation'. It is a call based on the fact that that is what God is about: reconciling the world to Godself. There is a self-confidence in this Pauline assertion that can be unsettling at first sight. The new creation is not necessarily a dif-ferent you: it is a 'you' that knows one's limitations and foibles and acknowledges them and thus speaks not from a superiority complex but from a humility that declares that Christ is one's righteousness. On that basis proclamation is not about 'holier than thou' but about proclaiming Christ's righteousness which then shines through one, albeit 'in a glass darkly' (1 Corinthians 13), with the confidence that one is reflecting Christ from one degree of glory to another. A bishop in mission is such a one.

Insight: What does the bishop see?

The Bible speaks of the word of God as something that is both seen and heard and then proclaimed. God's messengers, the proph-ets (in the Old Testament), are also known as seers. They saw before they spoke. They were both foretellers and forth-tellers. They told of things to come as well as of things present. They spoke of the here and now. They spoke about what they saw. They spoke about their visions, dreams and insights into cur-rent situations. God often asked the prophet about what he saw and then gave him a word from it for God's people. Even those who recorded the prophecies sometimes began by saying 'this is the word/oracle of God that the prophet so and so saw'. The prophets were given a peek into God's mind! This gave them the content of their proclamation. The New Testament continues in the same vein with regard to the apostles. A qualification for one to be an apostle was that one must have seen Jesus. An apostle is one who is sent, a herald of tidings. The content of those tidings is Jesus the Christ. As the writer of the first letter of St John says 'That which we preach to you is that which we have seen and

59

touched and experienced' (1 John 1.1–4). Not hearsay but first-hand knowledge. These requirements are no less for the successors of the apostles. In this sense, then, the bishop as a leader in mission must have seen the vision of God. He or she must have firsthand experience of the saving God before he or she can presume to be an evangelist and an apostle. The bishop is one who sees with the eyes of faith. They see before everyone else has any clue. They have to be a visionary. In the case where this is lacking the prayer of Paul for the Ephesians becomes one that the Church ought to pray for their bishop. They must pray that 'the eyes of his or her heart must be opened so that he may see the riches of the glory to which he has been called together with the saints' (Eph. 1.15–23). The bishop is therefore a person of faith as the writer to the Hebrews says: 'faith is the vision of things not seen, things yet to be'. They are ones who see things into being by the help of the Spirit of God. A closer reading of Luke 9 and 10 helps illustrate what this may look like. One can either see (or hear) *harvest* in this passage or one can see and hear the *work/labour* that is to be done. A bishop who seriously engages in the mission of God will not read the labour but will focus on the harvest that is to be. This is why I think Jesus does not begin that passage by highlighting the labour but highlights the harvest: 'the harvest is plentiful . . .'. It is about how you *look* at it. This is the attitude of a person who has a heart for church growth. This is not about satisfaction that all logistical requirements have been made before a new diocese is born. This is where the missionary diocese idea comes from. It is the vision of a diocese that is yet to be. This type of vision is not hallucination but faith and obedience to what is seen with the eyes of faith. As the prophet says, 'Where there is no vision people perish!' (Prov. 29.18) The bishop would need to be an Elijah type of visionary who saw the rain cloud when nobody else could see it. A stubbornness of some kind is required in this theological principle. It is not a wish but a proclamation of what God has revealed to the bishop. As can be seen this presupposes such a relationship with God that one would risk being known as stubborn. It may not be far-fetched to imagine that this is the faith that the missionary pioneers of all ages had and still have. Many a diocese in Africa has come into being this way as quite a number of African bishops can testify.

Insight is not only about sneak previews into God's designs. It is also about seeing into situations. Many missionaries have gone into situations they did not understand and pontificated against worldviews they found. Those of us from non-western parts of the Communion have felt this acutely and are still hampered from full expression of our experiences of God because of this kind of attitude. Any bishop, anywhere, would need to have some insights into the people and places where they are placed. Insight is seeing from the inside. Syncretism and split Christianity seems to be a lot of our people's experiences. They operate in two worldviews. There are two ways of understanding this. One is that what is considered syncretism is just the perception of the viewer who is speaking from their worldview. The other is over-zealous accommodation (or is it political correctness?) that will not condemn real syncretism because the insight is lacking. By split Christianity I mean a 'Jekyll and Hyde' type of double faith in which one dabbles in both Christian and non-Christian behaviour and faith expression depending on where one is or what one is doing at the time. A lot of damage has been done due to blanket condemnation of things not understood. In some cases the gospel has been misunderstood or is not expressed adequately due to inadequate idiom and symbols. Had local idiom and symbolisms been employed they would have expressed the gospel better than forced foreign (usually western) idioms being employed. Insight into particular local cultures which aids proper sensitivities is a helpful attitude for a bishop who practises mission. This is one of the major challenges in the formation of clergy and the teaching of theology in general in some parts of the Communion. A process of recovery is under way in some parts and in others it is considered suspect and a possible hindrance to complete reception of the gospel. At the same time, proper insight into cultures helps in the ability to recognize and name evil for what it is. This is also the challenge of the New Age Movement and other forms of postmodernity that extol relativity.

There are times when political correctness is not an ally of the proclamation of the gospel. The eyes of a bishop with insight are always open to the vision of the Glory of God and the manifestation of evil and their mind has the wherewithal for the discernment and discrimination required. A univocal proclamation (in favour of the dominant hegemonic insight) lingers dangerously on the brink of a Tower of Babel disaster.

Linguist: What does the bishop say?

Here I am not talking about being multilingual, even though that is immensely helpful. Does the bishop communicate well or is the way he speaks a hindrance to the proclamation of the Good News? Since proclamation has to do with interpretation does the bishop have the skill to make the gospel plainly understood? An effective missionary bishop is one who can understand the language of the times and be able to interpret it to his people. He is one who can also speak to it. Even though one may not want to push the matter of actual languages one cannot ignore the fact that it is immensely helpful for a bishop to be able to speak the language of the people for whom he has oversight. Not only is this important for bishops, it is important for all involved in God's mission. One other expression of our proclamation is that of links and exchanges. More often than not those of us from the South speak a language from the North/West, and we are required to have mastered it to be able to live and work – let alone be allowed in – in those countries. The same is not required vice versa. This, I believe, is a disservice to the proclamation of the gospel. Both sides are guilty of this: those of us who do not require it of those coming over to our part of the Communion and those who do not make their missionaries learn the language before they go out.

One of the many ways in which the bishop speaks is in the context of the liturgy. He must be at home in religious language and also in the regular idiom of the people. The celebration of the liturgy speaks more than words since liturgy uses a lot of symbols.

Many a time people have attended services in languages that they do not understand but have come out having understood everything that was going on in the liturgy. This may be out of familiarity with the liturgy but it has more to do with symbol. A bishop who is worth his salt must be one who takes seriously and requires of his clergy to take seriously the celebration of the liturgy. A well-celebrated liturgy gives us a glimpse of heaven! And what an evangelistic tool it is. In Malawi we have had experiences of people converting to Anglicanism from other faiths and from other Christian traditions through their experience of a marriage service or a funeral service. This is more than the fact that the sermon may be good. It tends to be that the liturgy elicits reverence and awe from them. Those of us from an Anglo-Catholic background have learnt from the evangelical tradition the power of open-air crusades. A bishop who is in the business of church growth cannot undervalue this activity. If he is not himself a gifted crowd mover he does well to appear at these events even if only to open and close the event. This speaks volumes to the evangelists but also to the faithful and the converts. Sometimes the crusades have been seen as the domain of the new Christian movements. It is amazing what happens when a mainline church religious leader like a bishop appears at these in official capacity. Not only does he receive respect but his presence tends to enhance the preached word at the event. This sounds like presumption but it is not. This just goes to show the power of ecumenical approach to proclamation. Initiatives like the *Transformation* movement (with its World Day Prayer every Pentecost Day) which has become a worldwide phenomenon have become powerful times of prayer and proclamation because bishops have humbled themselves to participate in what has been the domain of the less respectable Christian movements. Strange bedfellows indeed! I say strange because for the most part the new movements have tended to disparage the witness of the more established churches. This is helping in breaking down barriers in cooperation in the gospel and the benefits have been immense, especially among the young. A bishop who is seen to care about the things that the young are interested in and their ways of worship earns the trust of the young and when he speaks they listen. A bishop who speaks in this way conveys the divine fiat. His words speak participation and new creativeness and new life into being in the Church. The bishop is freed from enslavement to any particular churchmanship. The mission of God requires flexibility, adaptability and malleability. These are the situations, when I have responded to the question about my churchmanship by saying that I am an Evangelical, Charismatic Anglo-Catholic. There is a theological crassness and shallowness in this expression and yet it does illustrate the point. Neither Apollos nor Cephas nor whoever matters, only Christ crucified.

Exemplar: How does the bishop live it?

Words, words, meaningless words! The foregoing begs the question of whether the bishop can walk the talk. St Francis has been quoted as having said that we should 'preach always and if necessary use words'. The mere fact that the bishop was in a parishioner's house is big news for that family. It is as if God himself has visited them. This may sound very much like idolizing the bishop but it is not. The bishop's ministry of presence cannot be overstated. Just as the master himself became human so the bishop's ministry of presence with his people and those who least expect it speaks volumes of the Good News. There was none too low for Christ to touch and visit, none too rich for him to notice. The lepers and the unclean of all sorts found a listener and a saviour in him. This is what proclamation looks like in matters of reconciliation and in situations of HIV and AIDS. Where stigma abounds the care and welcome that comes from the Church and more especially the bishop brings healing and hope.

In places like Malawi and other disaster-prone areas the fact that a bishop and his team respond to the needs of the people with relief supplies regardless of religious affiliation or lack thereof speaks of the loving and caring God. These works of mercy preach; more so if they are not intentionally used as means for coercion to one's church. People know when they are being used and when they are being enticed. We have heard this from the traditional leaders in the areas where we work as they tell us their experiences of other actors in their plight. Not only have testimonies come from traditional leaders, they have come also from local political leaders who have seen and experienced our relief work. This is love not for gain but for the sake of the beloved. The example of Christ's self-sacrifice becomes the bench mark for the bishop and all who would be participants in God's ministry of proclamation.

Many a time bishops have regarded it as impossible to get to public ecumenical events which are not high profile. Usually this is mixing with those religious bodies whose stature is less than ours. A bishop has a gospel to proclaim and more often than not is more articulate than the others of 'lower' image. Pride of position would stand in the way of those others to drink of his or her fountain of wisdom. In places where bishops humble themselves they have led the way and opened opportunities, hitherto unknown, for multitudes to hear the gospel.

The bishop's vision and example of ministry is not something that should be hidden from others. The Apostle Paul had the audacity to tell his followers to imitate him as he imitated Christ. The bishop is an exemplar of what ministry and Christ-likeness is to be. Many people have been so disillusioned by examples of bad leadership and immorality of leaders that they have abandoned the faith. It is therefore of significant import that the bishop's behaviour and attitude preach a gospel, and that gospel had better be the gospel of Jesus Christ. Both clergy and laity look up to the exemplary proclamation of the Good News of Christ in the life of a bishop. It is not insignificant how a bishop lives his life. The bishop's life like that of his saviour should lead others to salvation.

It is not uncommon in our parts of the world where conflicts abound that it is the religious leaders to whom the people turn for mediation and reconciliation. Christ is our peace and has reconciled us to the Father and in so doing given us the ministry for reconciliation. This means that participation in the life of Christ is also participation in his ministry. Because the bishop does this well others want to be like him and even emulate him. Those so affected need the leadership and encouragement to grow into the full stature of Christ. The harvest is plentiful but the labourers are few.

Oversight: How does the bishop organize and facilitate it?

As said above, the bishop is only one person and the demands on his time are such that he cannot do it all. Oversight has to do with organization, facilitation and resourcing. Because of what the bishop sees, says and exemplifies it becomes imperative for him to make sure that the proclamation happens. In every diocese in the Communion, as part of its fabric, the work of evangelism is done either by establishing desks with officers or by other means. Certainly there is no shortage of programmes of church growth and outreach. As is evident from the foregoing there is an assumption that this happens naturally. Indeed this is the case in many places. However, most of us have to learn; as the prophet Isaiah says of the servant of God, he is one who is taught of God and day by day sits as a learner. Not only does the bishop need to learn but he also needs to make sure that his people and those so gifted and so called to this ministry are trained. The Anglican Communion is so blessed to have mission agencies of all kinds whose job is to facilitate this work. Knowing how to access them and utilizing them to the fullest possible degree is a good use of the gifts of God to the Communion. There are also resources which have been produced by Communion-wide consultation such as the reports of MISAG, MISSIO (Mission Commission of the Anglican Communion) and IASCOME (Inter Anglican Standing Commission on Mission and Evangelism) and some by the mission agencies. Partnerships in the link diocese programme mean that there is a plethora of possibilities in the mutual sharing and responsibility, as was articulated in the Toronto Anglican Congress of 1963 and record as *Mutual Responsibility and Interdependence*. The gifts that we all have from the Lord are not only for our benefit, they are primarily for the edification of the body. The bishop who is also the chief teacher and shepherd of the flock of God understands that the gifts are given for the equipping of the saints (Ephesians 4). What happens more often than not is that these resources, mentioned above, lie on bishops' shelves without being used for resourcing and equipping the saints. Good stewardship requires the use of these resources.

Following the Lambeth Conference of 1978 renewal became a familiar term in the Communion to the extent that the Anglican Renewal Ministry was born in various parts of the Communion. This movement of the Spirit was no respecter of churchmanship. It blew among both the Evangelicals and the Anglo-Catholics. The Spirit of God blows where he wills. This led in later years to the formation of the Sharing of Ministries Abroad (SOMA). The expression that is used more frequently these days about mission is 'mission by everyone from everywhere to everywhere'. The bishop's role is thus one of mobilization, training and deploying everyone to everywhere. One of the emphases laid by Brian McLaren, during his address to the Lambeth Conference 2008, was that evangelism is well and good but if it does not produce disciples it falls short of its intended purpose. The so-called great commission in Matthew 28 makes this point clear: 'Go . . . and make disciples.' Admittedly this is one of the challenges of fast growing churches. The preaching spreads so fast and does not keep pace with the training of disciples and teachers to nurture the new converts. Evangelism and all proclamation is not an end in itself. It is for the making of disciples who in turn become apostles (the sent ones) to the praise of God's glory. This is where the theology of the Church and the gifts of the Spirit, expressed in Ephesians 4, comes into its own. This passage, in my view, is a concise articulation of a theology of mission: initiated by God and enabled by the Spirit of God as the legacy of the Incarnate Christ's ascent with an explicit encouragement that this mission is already won; with captivity having been taken captive. The bishop who takes this understanding of mission seriously is indeed the encourager. Like the Chief Shepherd himself, the bishop knows his or her sheep by name, fends for and feeds them, goes out of his way to seek those that are lost and recognizes that there are also those that are not in the fold which need to be brought into it (John 10 and 17). All this is both the work and the fruit of proclaiming the Good News.

Conclusion

Proclamation of the News is carried out in complex contexts. The bishop is supposed to be leader of it. He or she speaks not his or her own message but that of the Father who sent him. He proclaims not him- or herself but Christ crucified. The bishop sees the creative Word of God and proclaims the transformation of unjust societies into being. He speaks not hearsay, but what he has seen and heard and experienced. In his work of oversight the bishop is the teacher, exemplar and encourager of all those who would participate in the mission of God. The bishop is thus an evangelist. The work of administration that the bishops do, they do in order to enable the proclamation of the Good News of Jesus Christ to happen. Jesus said, 'Just as the Father sent me so send I you.' The bishop, by the power of the Holy Spirit, is able to interpret the signs of the times and speak the truth of the gospel of Jesus Christ to a world that needs to be reconciled to the Father. Just as the bishop rejoices in the liturgy when he says that 'It is our bounden duty and our joy at all times and in all places to proclaim praises to the Father Almighty, Creator of heaven and earth,' he or she should in the same vein and in the same breath say that, like St John, he does the work of an evangelist so that his joy and that of his hearers may be complete.

4

TRANSFORMING
SOCIETY

The Bishop and Social Justice

Johannes T. Seoka

Introduction

'You will know the truth, and the truth will make you free' (John 8.32). The Church in our country has over the centuries been in the forefront of advocating for justice on behalf of the poor and powerless. Bishops saw it as their calling and mission to live the gospel and speak the truth to power. Some of the most dehumanizing laws in the world were practised under apartheid South Africa. Even today the remnants of these laws are a cause of mistrust and conflict between racial groups in our constitutional democracy.

Fifteen years into the new dispensation the gap between rich and poor has widened and deepened, and is the cause of frustration and conflict. The xenophobic violence that we have recently experienced is the result of a lack of service delivery and inequality. Millions of our people are still oppressed and exploited by the rich and powerful and this has to a large degree slowed development despite a flourishing economy. There are many similarities between the biblical story of the Israelites in Egypt and that of black people in apartheid South Africa. And the Church has not retired from engaging the powers and principalities of darkness through the work and leadership of bishops who know the truth and believe that the truth will set people free – 'You will know the truth, and the truth will make you free'(John 8.32).

It is the biblical knowledge of the truth that inspired the use of liberation theologies and social analysis to engage in the struggle for a just society. These hermeneutical tools empowered the church leaders and the Church to name the evil by its name – thus we boldly declared apartheid a heresy which had no theological justification as was claimed by Afrikaans theologians who supported the state policy of segregation. This was the kairos moment and South Africa was never the same again.

Church and social justice work: A perspective

The inextricable link between the church leadership structures, and the political and social dimensions in which these are situated, has long been recognized in the Anglican Communion, albeit in various forms and to various degrees. It has been understood that logical and consistent discipleship must carry with it a willingness to engage in the political narrative. Thus, witness to salvation must belong in all of the dimensions of life (Moltmann: 1992), with the church leadership demanding not a politicizing of the Church, but rather an acceptance and a willingness to situate the Church within its socio-political context, and to engage actively within that context in order to bring about the kingdom of God.

This acceptance is reflected in two dominant theological narratives, namely the so-called Theology of Revolution and the Theology of Liberation, and some valuable insights are to be gained through brief consideration of these perspectives in their broadest senses. The first demands that the Church accepts its obligation to actively engage in the liberation of the poor and oppressed, with the poor and oppressed being read as all those who are alienated within our societies, for whatever reason, in whatever form. This is an obligation which, I will proceed to show, is firmly rooted in a deeply biblical foundation. This obligation and the willingness to participate in the radical transformation of our society becomes, in essence, an outward correspondence to humankind's inner spiritual journey of repentance – *regeneratio, reformatio* and *renovatio mundi* (Moltmann: 1992, p. 16). When read within this context, the revolutionary premises of the Bible are readily apparent – with themes of promise, exodus, resurrection and Spirit all emerging within a glorious context of hope and transformation. This is cogently captured by Sacks who notes that 'religious faith is central to a humane social order' (Sacks: 2005, p. 26), and again, 'faith lives not only in the privacy of the soul, but in compassion and justice' (Sacks: 2005, p. 27).

Spirituality in general, then, and our role as leaders within the Anglican Communion in particular, cannot direct itself only to the crucified Christ as a private and spiritualized matter, but must acknowledge at the deepest level that 'if the title "Christ" refers to the redeemer and liberator then "practical" Christian action can only be directed towards the liberation of man from his humanity' (Moltmann: 1974, p. 23).

In my reading and analysis of what Jesus said of himself in quoting the Isaiah prophecy in the synagogue where he was asked to read the Scriptures, 'The Spirit of the Lord is upon me, because he has anointed me to bring good news to the poor. He has sent me to proclaim release to the captives and recovery of sight to the blind, to let the oppressed go free, to proclaim the year of the Lord's favour' (Luke 4.18), this pronouncement defines who and what his mission in the world was all about. His mission seeks to liberate and to embrace every aspect of freedom from suffering, directing itself, inter alia, to the eradication of all forms of exploitation, violence and oppression, the elimination of racism and sexism from our communities, and the rejection of greed and corruption, down to faith's 'experience of liberation from the compulsion of sin and the eschatological hope of liberation from the power of death' (Moltmann: 1974, p. 17).

The premises reflected above must serve as the departure for our reflection on our own role as bishops in the transformation of our societies, and in the establishment of social justice. This reflection will give consideration to the associated biblical

injunctions underpinning the above, proceeding to a delibera-
tion on the Church as an instrument for societal transformation
through engagement, and of the involvement of the faithful in
advocating social justice.

Advocacy imperatives

The advocacy imperatives placed upon the office of the bishop
to enter into public discourse with a view to engaging in the
social justice narrative are manifold. One thinks of Paul's exhortation to the Romans that those who confess Jesus as the
Christ of God must not be conformed, but be transformed (Rom
12.2). According to Paul's teaching, transformation is a process
of change from within, first of an individual who, through this
process of transformation, becomes empowered as an agent of
change within the broader social context. Paul's exhortation is
as valid and relevant to us today as it was to the early Church.
The world as it is today often seems to no longer be a constructive place for human habitation and development. The need for
transformation of our society from a profane space characterized by oppression and enslavement in very form, to a sacred
space that affirms human dignity, is manifest. In order for such
radical change to happen, focused leadership is required, with
such leadership being clearly rooted in the Christ who is the
manifestation of God's purpose for creation. Here we can learn
about God's liberating power through such people as Moses
who led the Israelites from the bondage in Egypt to Canaan. As
bishops, it is our task to be agents of God's grace in the world,
a task which will only be carried out once we ourselves have
entered into a journey of personal inner spiritual transformation
of our own. It is fundamental to our mission as leaders that we
enter into a dynamic partnership with the large society of the
laity, seeking through dialogue and action to bring about the
reign of God within the broader socio-political structures, and
thus create a world in which God's will is done, as a foretaste
of heavenly life.

The Church which we lead is a community of faith. It is constituted by the laity who, in their different callings and capacities, need to be challenged through visionary leadership to engage as change agents in their respective capacities within the broader society. Together, laity and bishops are a community of transformation that lead the world in the constant prayerful enactment – 'Your will be done as it is in heaven'. The transformation of the world can only be brought about by those who are themselves transformed by the ongoing spiritual journey of renewal. No one, whether bishop, clergy or laity, will be in a position to take up the challenge to transform our world unless the process of inner transformation and renewal has taken place, and without the empowerment of the Holy Spirit, energized to strive for a better world that seeks justice and peace for all its inhabitants. This is the world we petition as we pray daily, 'Your kingdom come . . .' (Matt. 6.10ff.).

Amongst our many challenges as bishops, we are thus called to be peace builders and to strive for the realization of societies where justice and human dignity prevail. Research informs us that personal transformation is accomplished as people adopt and live the Micah challenge with one another – to act justly, show loving kindness, and walk humbly with God (Mic. 6.8). Such a lifestyle will, I contend, create an enabling and peaceful environment that sees the restoration of human dignity, and the prevalence of values of compassion and caring, because of rootedness in justice. It is therefore imperative that each person commits to capacitating others for a better quality of life, through a reflection on the gospel of Jesus Christ in seeking the realization of the kingdom of God, so that we are transformed, individually and collectively. This is critical, as it affirms irrevocably that the gospel is life-changing. Those who have heard it and embraced it cannot remain complacent with the status quo, either at a deeply personal level, or at the nexus between self and other. The gospel initiates and compels an ongoing journey of transformation for the better, a journey which resonates at every level of existence and action, and which allows for the realization of the kingdom of God in the world.

Biblical injunctions

This is given clear expression in the frequently cited Beatitudes of Matthew 5.1–12. Far from being 'pious platitudes' these are statements which issue a 'radical challenge to the contemporary religio-political situation' (Domeris: 1990, p. 67). These verses provide the pattern for the faithful, in their journey to seek the realization of the Reign of God. Reflecting on these verses, it is readily apparent that they address many of the complex social and political challenges facing the Anglican Communion today. The first four verses provide important insights to our leadership.

'Blessed are the poor in spirit, for theirs is the kingdom of heaven' (5.3). The gospel of the kingdom of God is proclaimed to the poor, and 'the future of the kingdom of God begins among the people who suffer most from acts of violence and injustice – and that is the poor' (Moltmann: 1990, p. 99). The poor includes all who are sick, crippled and homeless (Luke 14.21–23), the sad (Luke 6.21), and those who are enslaved and oppressed. Furthermore, in proclaiming the gospel to the poor, the judgement of God is proclaimed to the rich. Thus Jesus and his disciples, in proclaiming the message to the poor, do so in affirmation that the kingdom of God already belongs to the poor and the dispossessed; it does not merely summon to conversion and faith, it irrevocably discovers the kingdom of the poor, claiming this as God's kingdom. Reading both the Old and New Testaments one soon realizes that these are the people God came to liberate through Jesus as it was with Moses. Furthermore, sociologically, the Jesus movement in Galilee constituted a movement of the poor (Moltmann: 1990, p. 100) – the disciples were to go barefoot and possession-less and proclaim the gospel to the poor (Matt 6:25–30), and to share all that they had with 'everything in common', so that there was none in need among them (Acts 4.34–35).

This verse clearly illustrates the interplay between the gospel and the poor and dispossessed, who in turn are fundamental to the realization of the kingdom of heaven on earth. Furthermore, in real and practical terms, it demonstrates that our obligation as leaders of the Church is directed to those who are disempowered and dispossessed. 'Blessed are those who mourn, for they shall be comforted' (Matt 5.4). For those who heard this message at its first proclamation, death must have been a constant and very visible companion, not in its often sanitized form which it has come to assume in our own societies, but in all its rawness, brutality and harshness. We proclaim a Christ who is to be found in the midst of human degradation, and whose work is manifest in the graveyards of humanity; a God whose message affirms that where there is sorrow and loss, there he is also. The place of the Church is among the grief-stricken, and those who mourn, amongst those who suffer loss, and who are in despair.

'Blessed are the meek, for they shall inherit the earth' (Matt 5.5). Following Domeris (1990), this verse must be read in the context of Psalm 37.7, where the Hebrew word denoting meek, *oni*, denotes not only those who are humble and self-effacing, but those who are literally poor and oppressed, representing, with the proclamation by Jesus, the inauguration of a 'new age of justice and comfort and the realization of God's reign' (Domeris: 1990, p. 70).

'Blessed are those who hunger and thirst for righteousness.' This verse carries with it a weight of interpretations (Domeris: 1990, p. 70), being read variously as applying to those who are hungry or thirsty on account of their righteousness, or, alternatively, as those who hunger and thirst for a knowledge or experience of the righteousness of God. However, a third alternative presents itself: the translation may be rendered in such a manner as to denote not righteousness, but justice. Thus those who are blessed are those who, in the absence of justice, hunger and thirst.

Reflecting on the above, these four verses may be rendered as follows (Domeris: 1990, p. 71):

Blessed by God are those who are poor and stripped even of their spirit, for they will possess God's kingdom.

Blessed by God are those for whom brutal death is a constant companion, for God shall comfort them.

Blessed by God are those who have been oppressed, for they shall inherit God's land.

Blessed by God are those who hunger and thirst because there is no justice, for they will find justice.

Personal reflections: Africa and the realization of the Millennium Development Goals

In reflecting on the verses above, and on the imperative contained therein, I am mindful of my particular context, situated in the southern part of the African continent. The continent was once the centre of advanced learning, the pinnacle of development, and the repository of the very best cultural artefacts, accumulated over centuries. However, the ravages of colonialism and war have seen not only an enormous depletion of material resources, but also a decline in the quality of life and liberty of its inhabitants.

It is within this context that our role as bishops as agents of change and advocates of social justice becomes acutely important. The Southern African Development Community, within the structures of the African Union, has responded to the challenge of vigorously pursuing the realization of the Millennium Development Goals. However, given the historical depredation which the continent has suffered, the task is a mammoth one. The resolution adopted at the Lambeth Conference 2008 which gave recognition to the theological imperatives underpinning the Millennium Development Goals, and noting the necessity to clarify and state these imperatives more clearly, and to help each other to act upon these, is thus of particular significance within the African context.

Our role as bishops cannot be underestimated. The solutions derived through the pursuit of the Millennium Development Goals must, first and foremost, be representative of the collective will of the people of the continent, and must therefore seek to give voice to the social, economic, ideological and spiritual narratives of Africa.

I therefore see a particular obligation resting upon the bishops within the Southern African Development Community. Our voices must be heard on matters critical to the prosperity of the continent, and to the survivability and sustainability of Africa. The Millennium Development Goals, while representing a unique continental challenge, also pose an opportunity of note – an opportunity for the Church to truly demonstrate its character as a *Movement of the Poor* (Moltmann: 1990, p. 100).

South Africa and the interface between Church and society

The enormous transformative value to be found in embracing the dialectic between Church and society was brought home to me not so long ago. The community in which our diocese is situated was recently awakened to an unprecedented experience of xenophobic violence. Initially, as is so often the case, very few took notice of the devastating nature of this sudden inhuman attitude of South Africans towards those who were perceived as aliens/foreigners amongst them. The tragedy in this apathy was compounded by the reality that during our struggle for freedom, many South Africans sought refuge in the homelands of those very persons who were now the targets of xenophobic violence and persecution. The culmination of this xenophobia saw the tragic loss of lives of two foreigners, who were torched to death by a mob. This was indeed a wake-up call, as South Africans, with the rest of the world, watched the televised broadcasts of this atrocity, and grappled with the reality that this violence was taking place within our own society, and being perpetrated by our own people.

That morning marked a particular turning point for me in my own work of mission and ministry. I realized that as spiritual leaders and the disciples of Christ, we had neglected our calling to be shepherds of the flock of Christ which he entrusted to our love and care. The tragic situation demanded a collective response, and it was with this understanding that I gathered the church leaders of our city together, in order to visit the community where the death of the two foreigners had taken place. In making that visit, I observed once again that the perilous tendency of human beings to create exclusionary narratives and to marginalize each other though crude stereotyping was at play. I was mindful of the comment that

> It is easy for humans to stereotype one another . . . it is even easier for them to live out those stereotypes. Once we libel people, we go on about our lives feeling comfortable, since we have defined, analysed, and catalogued them – they have been captured and caged. (Ateek and Justice: 1989, p. 13)

This having been done, it is but a small step to the perpetuation of violence and atrocity. Conscience and collective morality is subsumed, as barbarism is justified.

As spiritual leaders, and mindful of our obligation to affirm always the fundamental message of the gospel, we were able to take a stand against the powers and principalities that undermined the human dignity in the 'stranger' amongst us, and honestly express our commitment to 'speak truth to power', acting justly against all forms of oppression, exploitation and violence against the weak and powerless. Our collective action provided a strong voice to the voiceless, and made visible in the media much which had hitherto been silenced. With the articulation of the concerns of the refugees, the authorities visited the site, and dialogue and engagement took place. As a result, security and basic necessities were provided, not only by the faith community, but also by broader non-governmental organizations within the diocese. There was deliberate effort from the Christians within the community to 'Act with justice and righteousness, and deliver from the hand of the oppressor anyone who has been robbed. And do no wrong or violence to the alien, the orphan and the widow, or shed innocent blood in this place' (Jer. 22.3). The faithful took it upon themselves to protect the strangers in their midst, with a concomitant easing of conflict and violence. The asylum seekers and refugees saw this as God's intervention through the church leaders, and they said, 'These are church and spiritual leaders whom we trust, because they are honest people.'

This instance brought home to me once again the enormous practical responsibility to be assumed by the leaders of the Church in addressing matters of social justice, and made real the assertion that 'many Christians look to their Church hierarchy to take the lead. They expect them to speak the truth without fear and to stand with the oppressed and marginalized, even if they have to suffer for it' (Ateek and Justice: 1989, p. 61). People of faith expect their bishops to lead, not only in terms of the traditional understanding of mission and ministry, but also to be in the forefront of the struggles of the people within their jurisdiction.

Of course, the story I have related above, and the actions taken within our diocese, are but one illustration of a well-established tradition within the province. Prior to the attainment of our democracy in 1994, the Church was instrumental in giving voice to the voiceless, and in furthering the struggle agenda in every sphere of society. As a province, we are mindful of the examples set by such icons of our liberation struggle as Archbishop Emeritus Desmond Tutu, whose efforts in leading an unrelenting campaign for justice and social transformation came to the attention of role players throughout the continent and within the international community, both in ecclesiastical and secular forums.

The actions of such church leaders as Archbishop Tutu, and many others before him, such as Archbishops Russell Darbyshire, Geoffrey Clayton and Joost De Blank, to mention but a few, who publicly defied the Apartheid government, provide an important illustration of the role of the bishop in transforming society and the Church's work of social justice, and serve to exemplify much of what I have said above.

Lessons for reflection

First, such actions and the effects thereof provide a clear illustration of the obligation of both bishops and lay leadership to participate in the transformation of their societies for the better, and in the liberation of the poor and the oppressed, in every sense.

Second, through such actions, the dialectic between the secular and the sacred is entered into, with the resultant shaping of the secular by the sacred. The participation by the Church in the work of social transformation and justice lends to these endeavours a far deeper and richer perspective, providing the context of the gospel of Jesus Christ. The implications of such a shaping process are considerable when one reflects upon the nature of our communities today. The aspirations and needs of the collective seem to have been displaced by a pursuit of the satisfaction of the needs of individuals; needs often driven by greed and individual competition. This loss of collective vision, and the reification of material symbols of wealth and status, have impacted upon our societies at every level, eroding the integrity of the family unit, and of the moral fabric upon which societies are founded. The so-called 'demoralization of discourse' (Sacks: 2005, p. 42) is readily in evidence. Never before has the need for the influence of the sacred space upon the secular, and often profane, been so acute. This is a task which faces the leadership of the Anglican Communion, and which confronts us as bishops in our respective spheres of influence.

Third, following the above, such action demonstrates clearly the link between 'theological concepts of conversion, repentance, new-birth and transformation on the one hand and the movement for social revolution . . . on the other', and that 'in order to mobilize and change people it is necessary to appeal to the emotional and rational sources of their identity and self-understanding – to their collective soul. This is largely a religious task' (Villa-Vicencio: 1990, p. 73). The call to conversion articulated by men and women such as Archbishop Tutu was without limitations. Thus such conversion must be seen as being as all-embracing as the coming kingdom of God, whose proclaimed closeness makes conversion possible and necessary. Like the discipleship of Christ, conversion takes place totally, holistically, 'with all the heart and with all the soul and with all the strength' (Deut 6:5) – like the love of God (Moltmann: 1990, p. 103).

Conclusion

There are good examples in the Anglican Communion of bishops who have provided leadership in the work of transformation and social justice. These are men and women who have in their Christian journey sought to live out the gospel teachings, and also to translate into practice the truth of Micah's words, 'to act justly, to love mercy and to walk humbly with [their] God'. I believe that it is the essence of the bishop's work of mission and ministry to promote justice for all. Lack or absence of justice is in most places the cause of conflict and wars.

In apartheid South Africa for instance the struggle for liberation was a response to oppressive laws and an education system that subjected black people to exploitation. In the early years of our Church many bishops and archbishops in the Province stood up against these injustices and paid the price as most of them were detained and ultimately deported. Their work made a difference because they collaborated with dedicated lay leaders within the Church. These men and women were the conscience of the nation and the voice of the voiceless during the dark ages of our country. Issues of racial discrimination, economic deprivation and unjust laws were major items on their agenda. They believed beyond doubt that apartheid and the deprivation of human rights were a violation of the gospel teachings which had to be opposed.

It was in the context of the struggle for human rights and social justice that the Bishop of Johannesburg, Geoffrey Clayton, said:

It is the business of the church to proclaim the principles laid down once and for all by the Head of the church, our Lord Jesus Christ . . . we claim no infallibility; but the principles themselves are eternally right, and it is the church's business to bear witness to them. And if we think that a policy which is being followed by a government, any government, runs counter to those principles, it is our duty to say so and to suggest a better way. We must do this whether men will hear or whether they will forbear. It is not our duty to be popular. It is our duty to be faithful and to refuse to be silenced. We must obey God rather than men. So beside our pastoral and missionary task we have a prophetic duty ... The Church as a whole must never allow itself to be tied to any political party. Whatever party is in power the church must try to follow its vocation to be the conscience of the nation ... The church must take a special care of the underprivileged and those who are prevented from speaking for themselves. If the church does not do this she is not true to her master. Yet that does not mean she should seek popularity among the poor ... I do not conceive it my duty as a minister to be a court chaplain to King Demos. Our Lord certainly was never that. (Clerk: 2008, p. 11)

After this citation, which I believe says it all, I need say no more as this is the classical example of the bishop's leadership in advocating social justice and speaking the truth to power for the sake of the kingdom of God.

Bibliography

Ateek, N. and Justice, S., *Justice: A Palestinian Theology of Liberation*, New York: Orbis Books, 1989

Clerk, B., *Anglicans Against Apartheid: 1936–1996*, Pietermaritzburg: Cluster Publications, 2008

Domeris, W., 'Exegesis and Proclamation' in *Journal of Theology for Southern Africa* 73, 1990, pp. 67–76

Moltmann, J., *The Church in the Power of the Spirit*, London: SCM Press, 1992

Moltmann, J., *The Way of Jesus Christ: Christology in Messianic Dimensions*, London: SCM Press, 1990

Moltmann, J., *The Crucified God*, London: SCM Press, 1974

Sacks, J., *The Persistence of Faith: Religion, Morality and Society in a Secular Age*, London: Continuum, 2005

Villa-Vicencio, C., 'Religion, Revolution and Reconstruction: The Significance of the Cuban and Nicaraguan Revolutions for the Church in South Africa' in *Journal of Theology for Southern Africa* 73, 1990, pp. 48–59

5

THE BISHOP, OTHER CHURCHES, AND GOD'S MISSION 1

Geoffrey Rowell

The section on ecumenism in the *Lambeth Indaba* report produced at the end of the 2008 Lambeth Conference rightly reminds us of the inseparable link between mission and unity.[1] In St John's Gospel the great High Priestly prayer of Jesus (John 17) focuses on the unity of his disciples. Their unity is to mirror and reflect the profound unity between Jesus and his Father. They are to be 'one as we are one'. It is this profound unity and communion for which we were made, and for that reason it lies at the root of mission. This communion is catholic and universal (open to all), but it is not a communion which is simply inclusive – to participate in this communion we have to respond to an invitation to universal transformation. Holiness and catholicity belong together and it is no accident that the High Priestly prayer of Jesus speaks of the interconnectedness of unity, communion and consecration. No less does it speak of mission, that apostolic note of the Church. The disciples of Jesus are to be one '*that the world may believe*'. As *Lambeth Indaba* puts it: 'Because the Church is divided its mission is impaired. Ecumenism, therefore, which seeks to make the Church one, is intimately and urgently

83

linked with that mission, and becomes a powerful route into the freedom which is displayed in the Lord's passion and resurrection and is for us the source of new life' (*Lambeth Indaba*, p. 24). When churches take unilateral actions which ignore this call to unity, and which lead to divergence rather than convergence, they are inevitably under judgement. Furthermore this prayer of Jesus is uttered in the context of his imminent betrayal and death. As Søren Kierkegaard sharply reminded us in his *Discourses at Communion*, communion was given and established by Christ out of the context of his betrayal. This sharp paradox at the very heart of the Church's life reminds us that ecumenical commitment is inseparable from discipleship and the sacramental life of the Church. It equally reminds us that such commitment is costly and that churches can continually betray the unity and communion which is the Lord's undoubted will.

Anglican identity cannot be divorced from the challenges posed to us by the sheer hindrance to mission caused by the disunity of Christians. Ecumenism is never something which is a specialist interest for those who like it. Unity is one of the marks of the Church, and no Christian can ignore the Lord's command. The *Lambeth Indaba* comments on Anglican identity that it is formed by Scripture, shaped by worship, ordered for communion and directed by God's mission, reminding us of the nature of the communion which both shapes us and which we are called to share.

> We have been brought by the redeeming work of Christ into a living communion with God and with all Christian people in our baptism. This communion, which mirrors the life of the Holy Trinity, is God's gift to the Church, which our human structures only inadequately reflect and sustain. The Anglican Communion shares a particular history within the one holy catholic and apostolic Church and that history brings us into a particular relationship with one another. (*Lambeth Indaba*, p. 37)

The communion which we already share with Christians of other churches is an expression of our common baptism, which binds us together in the common life of the body of Christ. The Eucharist sustains, nurtures, feeds and shapes us in that same communion, and so Anglicans have never been content with a baptismal ecclesiology; we need also a eucharistic ecclesiology. That eucharistic theology has a sacrificial note because in 'doing this', making Eucharist in obedience to the Lord's command, in the powerful words of the ARCIC agreed statement on the Eucharist, 'we enter the movement of His self-offering'.[2] Likewise the Eucharist does not only look backward in recalling the mighty acts of redemption, and does not only make these present realities, it looks to the future consummation. As St Paul reminds us, 'as often as we eat this bread and drink this cup we show the Lord's death until he comes' (1 Cor. 11.26). The 'daily bread', for which we ask in the Lord's Prayer, is most likely the bread of the Day of the Lord, the Feast of Heaven which we ask to share in here and now.[3]

The Communion to which we are committed is full, visible unity. Many churches and ecclesial traditions have regarded a federal model as a sufficient goal for the unity to which Christ calls us. Anglicans have disagreed, as they have also taken issue with Christians who have been content to speak of an invisible unity. The incarnational emphasis of much Anglican theology means that full, visible (or organic) unity is that for which we must seek to live and strive. The *Lambeth Indaba* reaffirmed 'the commitment of the Anglican Communion to the full visible unity of the Church now'. As that combative figure of the Oxford Movement, W. G. Ward, once commented, 'an invisible church would be a very sorry antagonist against so very visible a world' (Ward: 1889, p. 147).

It is not surprising therefore that successive Lambeth Conferences have devoted much attention to ecumenism and the relations between the churches of the Anglican Communion and other churches. Ten years ago at the Lambeth Conference of 1998 Ecumenical Relations was one of the four major sections of the Conference and there were a series of resolutions passed concerned with ecumenical relations. It was from the same 1998 Conference that encouragement was given to bring into being a

Commission charged with an overview of the relation between the Communion and other churches so that there was a coherence between what Anglicans were saying, for instance, to Lutherans in North America, in Africa, in Scandinavia and the Baltic countries, and in Germany. The Commission thus established, the Inter-Anglican Standing Commission for Ecumenical Relations (IASCER),[4] has met regularly each year under the chairmanship of Archbishop Drexel Gomez of the West Indies and has proved itself to be a valuable forum for analysing and evaluating the ecclesiological issues that arise between the churches, and to review and comment on ecumenical agreements, and to identify issues that were liable to hinder rather than help the search for full visible unity, the goal to which Anglicans have been historically committed, which was reaffirmed by Lambeth 1998 and endorsed by Lambeth 2008.[5] Resolutions of IASCER have been regularly published on the Anglican Communion website and forwarded to the ACC (Anglican Consultative Council), enabling the ecumenical consequences of actions in one part of the Communion to be clearly noted and recognized. I have been a member of IASCER since its inception, latterly serving as Vice-Chair. Not only has IASCER proved to be one of the few standing theological groups serving the Communion, it has developed a method of theological reflection which has served the Communion well and enabled significant resolutions and comments to be put to both the primates and the ACC. Inevitably the issues of ecumenical dialogue and conversation because they concern ecclesiology and differences and convergences in Faith and Order also touch on issues that are matters of tension, concern and debate within the Communion. It is partly the recognition of this fact that has led to the suggestion that, following IASCER's final meeting in Kyoto in December 2008, a new commission should be formed which will have an explicit mandate of addressing both ecumenical concerns and issues of Faith and Order. It is to be hoped that any new commission will not lose the vision, trust and working together which has characterized IASCER.

Because Lambeth 2008 was shaped so very differently from previous Lambeth Conferences it can be argued that the ecumenical dimension embodied in Section E of *Lambeth Indaba* was considerably weaker than the ecumenical contributions of previous conferences. Although the authority of Lambeth Conferences has never been juridically binding,[6] it has undoubtedly had a significant moral authority. This has arguably grown over the century and a half that Lambeth Conferences have met. In the ecumenical sphere it should be noted that Lambeth Conferences have approved the Chicago–Lambeth Quadrilateral and the ARCIC *Final Report*. Endorsement by the Lambeth Conference has been the way in which the Communion as a whole has been able to give consent to such a significant ecumenical agreement. Consequently if the authority of the Lambeth Conference has been weakened then it can clearly be argued that past ecumenical commitments have inevitably been weakened. Lambeth Conferences have been the vehicle of a Communion wide endorsement of significant ecumenical dialogue with other churches; the approval of the *Final Report* of ARCIC is a notable case in point. It is to be regretted that the absence of any voting and resolutions from Lambeth 2008 effectively precluded any similar ecumenical commitment. The important documents from The International Anglican–Roman Catholic Commission for Unity and Mission (IARCCUM), *Growing Together in Unity and Mission*, and the Cyprus Statement of the Anglican–Orthodox International Theological Dialogue, *The Church of the Triune God*, were offered as important resources to the 2008 Conference, but were unable to be received and approved. Likewise the agreed statement on Christology of the Anglican–Oriental Orthodox Joint Doctrinal Commission, which it had been hoped would have received the approval of the Conference, could not structurally be received. By the same token the question of 'overlapping Anglican jurisdictions' in Europe, which had been specifically mandated by the 1998 Conference for a progress report in 2008, could not be considered in the way anticipated in 1998. Although there were proper concerns raised about the abundance of resolutions, and the difficulty attending some of them in 1998, it is almost certainly true that not to have any mechanism of allowing the gathered bishops of the Anglican Communion to endorse significant ecumenical statements has weakened the Communion's ability to make a considered commitment to ecumenical agreements. Such commitment has in the past been regarded as binding on the Communion as a whole.

The 2008 Lambeth Conference was, as previous Lambeth Conferences have been, enhanced by the presence of a significant number of ecumenical guests. As with previous Conferences there was a distinction between those from churches in communion, (such as the Old Catholics, the Mar Thoma Church in India, and the Independent Philippine Church, and the churches of the Porvoo communion in Northern Europe in communion with the Anglican churches in Britain and Ireland), and other ecumenical partners, notably the Roman Catholic, Orthodox, and Oriental Orthodox churches, together with representatives of the Lutheran churches, the World Alliance of Reformed Churches, and the Baptist Union and others. They were welcomed as participating partners and not simply as observers, and in this connection it is worth recalling a powerful phrase once used to me by the Roman Catholic Archbishop in Belgrade, when I asked him if there was a possibility of the Archdeacon of the Eastern Archdeaconry of the Diocese in Europe attending a particular conference of Roman Catholic bishops in South-East Europe as an observer. The archbishop replied in a powerful phrase that 'When Christians meet there are no observers.' Thus at Lambeth 2008 Cardinal Dias gave a powerful address on mission and evangelism, and Cardinal Kasper, President of the Pontifical Council for Christian Unity, attended for a significant number of days, participated in one of the *indaba* groups and gave an important paper on Anglican–Roman Catholic relations to one of the 'self-select' groups. It was in that context that Cardinal Kasper was asked by the Archbishop of Canterbury to describe the Anglican Communion he would like to see, to which he replied there were three things he would like to see – 'a Communion once more securely grounded in Scripture and the Fathers; a re-reception of Holy Orders; and a new Oxford Movement'. It is a reminder that when Cardinal Kasper addressed the Church of England College of Bishops on the subject of women bishops his argument on bishops in relation to the unity of the

Church was built very much on the ecclesiology of St Cyprian as an ecclesiology to which Anglicans have historically appealed.[7]

The *Lambeth Indaba* report notes that 'current divisions between Anglicans and the actions by certain provinces that have provoked them have inevitably disrupted not only the internal life of the Communion but also ecumenical dialogues and cooperation. Our ecumenical partners are sometimes bewildered by apparent Anglican inconsistency especially where issues of authority and ecclesiology are concerned' (*Lambeth Indaba*, p. 24). There is no doubt that the consecration of Gene Robinson as a bishop, not only divorced but in a committed same-sex relationship, had significant repercussions on Anglican ecumenical dialogue, particularly with the Roman Catholic and the Oriental Orthodox Churches, and caused strained relations with the Russian Orthodox Church in particular. The IARCCUM document *Growing Together in Mission and Unity* had originally been intended to move more in the direction of a common statement of faith rather than a document harvesting some of the fruits of the ARCIC conversations and pointing towards a greater degree of cooperation in mission. The Robinson consecration put a hold on this direction, and resulted in the end in what was an important, but less significant, document which was accorded a lesser status. It also raised sharply the question as to whether the Communion as a whole is or is not committed to such an endorsement of same-sex relationships as compatible with the gospel and how that sat with Anglican claims to be grounded in Scripture and Tradition.

Another consequence of the Robinson consecration was the suspension of the fruitful dialogue with the Oriental Orthodox Churches. The Commission had been due to hold its second meeting in England, following an earlier meeting in Holy Etchmiadzin, Armenia, in which a major Christological agreement had been reached. As Anglican co-chair of the Commission I had been looking forward to engagement on the theme of the Holy Spirit, both the question of the *filioque* and papers from the two families of churches on 'the life of the Holy Spirit in the Church'. The meeting was scheduled for the week which proved to be that in which the consecration of Gene Robinson was to happen, and on the Friday evening preceding it I received a call from Catholicos Aram, the Armenian Catholicos of Cicilicia, informing me that as a result of a meeting with the Syrian Orthodox Patriarch and Pope Shenouda of the Coptic Church, they had decided that it was not the time to be talking to Anglicans. The meeting of the commission was therefore aborted. It has not to date proved possible to restart this dialogue, though significant conversations towards this end have been had, not least during the Archbishop of Canterbury's visit to Armenia, Syria and Lebanon in 2007. It is a salutary reminder that not only within the Communion but within our ecumenical relationships we are members one of another, and sacramental actions have ramifications which reach out far beyond the particularities of a particular church or province. Again this poses sharply the question of Anglican identity, ecclesiology and authority. The question ecumenical partners rightly ask is, 'With whom is it that we are in dialogue? To whom are we talking? What precisely are the limits of apparent Anglican diversity?' Anglicans who have not been party to, and who have not been consulted about, the actions of a particular province, which have serious implications for the quest for Christian unity, can be rightly aggrieved when ecumenical dialogue is thus unilaterally disrupted. Boundaries can appear to be pushed as to what is, and what is not, within the boundaries of Anglican faith, polity and commitment to holiness of life.

Those concerned with ecumenical dialogue are well used to the patient processes by which common statements are agreed. The ARCIC method of endeavouring to go back behind the polemical language and stances of previous divisions to seek a common understanding – the ARCIC Agreed Statement on the Eucharist famously relegates transubstantiation (a way of expressing Christian belief in the Real Presence of Christ in the Sacrament in terms of Aristotelian philosophy) – has been followed in a number of other dialogues: e.g., the Anglican–Oriental Orthodox agreed statement on Christology builds on a common statement between the Chalcedonian Byzantine churches and the non-Chalcedonian Oriental Orthodox Churches, together with joint statements by the Pope and Oriental Orthodox Patriarchs, and an Oriental Orthodox–Reformed common statement; and the Porvoo conversations seek to find ways of understanding the sign of the historic episcopate in apostolic succession, recognizing a succession in faith, teaching and historic see, as well as the tactile sign of the laying on of hands. In this context of ecumenical dialogue there is a familiarity with common statements and ecumenical agreements. This context makes the work towards an Anglican Covenant entirely understandable, and there is no doubt that the proposal for an Anglican Covenant, as expressed in the *Windsor Report*, has certainly been welcomed by the Roman Catholic Church, as well as by other ecumenical partners. If we can articulate a common faith with Christians of other traditions we should surely be able to do it amongst ourselves, particularly at a time when other Christians with whom we are deeply engaged in the journey to realizing the full visible unity which Christ willed for his Church are asking sharp questions about the boundaries and limits of Anglican diversity, and about the identity of those with whom they are in dialogue. Bishops, who are called to be the focus of unity, need to take that ecumenical context and journey seriously. And because what we say and do ecumenically flows from and impacts on our Anglican self-understanding, a commitment to relations with other churches carries with it a commitment to Anglican identity. And in this context we need to note what is said in *Lambeth Indaba*: 'The Anglican Communion has never seen its life as a family of Churches as self-sufficient, nor does it claim any universal identity other than as a part of the One Holy Catholic and Apostolic Church' (*Lambeth Indaba*, p. 24). When a province of the Anglican Communion fails to recognize the bonds that bind it to the rest of the Communion, division and conflict result. By the same token Anglicans are bound by common ties with those with whom we share a common baptism, a common confession of the apostolic faith in the catholic creeds, and in a particular way with those churches with whom Anglicans have always claimed to share in common the historic apostolic ministry; unilateral actions have similar consequences in relation to other churches as they do in relation to the Communion as a whole.

Lambeth Indaba is right to insist, as we have already noted, that 'current divisions between Anglicans and the actions by certain provinces that have provoked them have inevitably disrupted not only the internal life of the Communion but also ecumenical dialogues and co-operation' (*Lambeth Indaba*, p. 24). What ecumenical partners often see as they look at the current situation in the Anglican Communion is an Anglican inconsistency which focuses particularly on unresolved tensions around the issues of authority and ecclesiology. The recent decision by the Synod of the Archdiocese of Sydney in the Anglican Church of Australia, that deacons and licensed laity may preside at Holy Communion, subverts what has been a common Anglican position in relation to eucharistic presidency, and will therefore again cause ecumenical partners to question the integrity of Anglicans who have signed ecumenical commitments where only those ordained as priest or bishop may preside at the Eucharist. It is not only matters of sexual morality which can undermine ecumenical convergence.

Ecumenical dialogues are important, and the theological convergence revealed in the many ecumenical texts of ARCIC, the Anglican–Orthodox dialogue, and the dialogues between Anglicans and Lutherans in many parts of the world provide a rich resource for Anglican theological reflection. It is good that the *Lambeth Indaba* conversations noted the importance of ecumenical activity at a local level, even going so far as to suggest that the future of ecumenism might be 'from the bottom up and not top down', with the qualification, however, that 'whatever we do at local level must accord with dialogue at the top' (*Lambeth Indaba*, p. 29). Likewise it was important that one of the most essential ingredients of good ecumenical relations was underlined – 'relationships, especially between Christian leaders'. 'Bishops, therefore must be leaders involved in local ecumenism, standing together with leaders of other denominations in the proclamation of the Gospel, and the empowerment of the Church in its mission and witness' (*Lambeth Indaba*, p. 30). Jesus said to his disciples that he called them friends, and friendship is something that reaches across the barriers of tradition and builds and enables trust under the understanding of one another's stories.

Churches need each other, and Christian division not only hampers Christian mission, but leaves churches with particular deficits. As the recent controversies and tensions within the Anglican Communion have clearly demonstrated there is an ecclesial deficit in Anglicanism in relation to the ability of Anglicans to speak with a common voice as a global communion. It is not surprising that questions about primacy have been raised within Anglicanism, both in relation to the office and ministry of the Archbishop of Canterbury, and to the Primates' Meetings. The latter came into existence in order to address the need for consultation between the churches of the Communion in between Lambeth Conferences. The Archbishop of Canterbury has been looked to for guidance in conflictual situations which have had the inevitable effect of enhancing his ministry and office. And it needs to be remembered that the Archbishop of Canterbury is one of only three Christian leaders who have a global ministry by virtue of office, the others of course being the Pope and the Ecumenical Patriarch. Although Anglicans have been sensitive to the Roman Primacy, and have no desire to replicate the papacy, it is not for nothing that questions concerning primacy are on the Anglican agenda. The very fact that ARCIC could consider the need for a universal primacy in *The Gift of Authority* shows a significant openness to a Petrine office serving the unity of the universal Church. That same ARCIC report also underlined the importance of synodality as an Anglican gift to the Church universal, though the particular forms that takes in the General Synod of the Church of England or the General Convention of the Episcopal Church are not thereby being endorsed, for they are far from perfect instruments of church governance.

The ecumenical imperative raises critical questions of ecclesiology, our understanding of the identity and character of the Church, and authority within it. These are the same questions raised by the present tensions within the Anglican Communion which the structure of the 2008 Lambeth Conference was designed to enable us to address. When we seek to resolve these issues we cannot afford to ignore other churches, and heed what they are saying to us. It is vital to our mission, for we are called to be one that the world may believe.

GEOFFREY ROWELL

Bibliography

Ward, Wilfrid, *William George Ward and the Oxford Movement*, London: Macmillan and Co., 1889

Notes

1 *Lambeth Indaba: Capturing Conversations and Reflections from the Lambeth Conference 2008 – Equipping Bishops for Mission and Strengthening Anglican Identity*, pp. 23–4, 29–30. Available online at http://www.lambethconference.org/reflections/document.cfm

2 The text of this 1971 statement can be found at www.prounione. urbe.it/dia-int/arcic/eucharist.html

3 Cf. Geoffrey Wainwright, *Eucharist and Eschatology*, London: Epworth, 1971.

4 *Lambeth Indaba*, p. 31, 'Resources', where it is noted that 'the establishment of the Inter Anglican Standing Commission on Ecumenical Relations (IASCER) was endorsed at the Lambeth Conference of 1998 to monitor and enable Anglican participation in ecumenical activity and to ensure consistency of approach'.

5 *Lambeth Indaba*, §71 Ref. Resolution IV.1, Lambeth Conference 1998.

6 As is well known this was in major part because the Established character of the Church of England and its particular position in relation to the British State could not yield a jurisdictional authority to an external body. This same issue has been already highlighted by the present legal adviser to the General Synod of the Church of England, Stephen Slack, in a paper setting out difficulties which may face the Church of England in acceding to any Anglican Covenant, desirable though that may be on other grounds.

7 Some of the Church of England's responses to and reflections on Cardinal Kasper's address can be found in James Rigney (with Mark D. Chapman), *Women as Bishops*, London: Mowbray, 2008, pp. 110–23. The text of the Cardinal's address can be found at http://www.cofe. anglican.org/news/pr6006b.html. There were in fact four different responses, all given in an official document. This has caused puzzlement to a number of Roman Catholics, for whom such official diversity is a problem, and it may also be said to raise questions of ecclesial coherence for Anglicans.

6

THE BISHOP, OTHER CHURCHES, AND GOD'S MISSION 2

John William Hind

That bishops and churches (or better, churches and bishops) only exist in relation to God's mission should go without saying. Without getting into futile discussions about whether or how far Jesus directly instituted the Church as we know it or, more importantly, confess it in the Creed, it is obvious that the Church and its structures must be faithful to, reflect or embody the Good News of God in Christ. At least, they must do so if they are to be accounted 'Christian' in any meaningful sense at all. The Lord's own words, 'As the Father sent me, even so do I send you,' must be a permanent aspect of the self-understanding of his commissioned ministers throughout the ages, and is one (albeit only one) aspect of what it means to be apostolic.

Unfortunately from Diotrephes (3 John) to the present day some bishops and other leaders of Christ's faithful have shown themselves to be all too ready to see themselves as and to act as imperial legates, as feudal barons or as executives of corporate bodies and as guardians of its real estate – almost anything, that is, other than as pastors of Christ's flock. No early twenty-first-century Anglican readers of this essay will miss the import of this observation!

Over the early Christian centuries the Church itself began to be seen as an institution more in a sociological than a theological sense. This was an early, significant and not very helpful development. Decisive watersheds were reached when, early in the fourth century, the Roman Emperor Constantine first tolerated and then patronized Christianity, and when at the end of the same century the Emperor Theodosius established the faith as the official religion of the Empire. From then on the Church's structures and officers belonged and were answerable to not only the Church but also the secular authorities.

A century and a quarter before Constantine, however, Tertullian had spoken of the *institutum*, meaning by this term 'what God has done in Christ and its effects in history'. He did not primarily mean an organization in the way the modern world describes it.

Nonetheless, what was instituted by Christ had to find 'institutional' expression; indeed, more than expression, it needs to have means and instruments. So it was that, as St Leo the Great was to write, 'what was visible in the incarnation has passed into the sacraments'. For Leo and his contemporaries this had to be understood in relation to the Church of which the sacraments were a constitutive part. The expression 'the Eucharist makes the Church' may be modern, but it articulates a fundamental truth – always to be balanced by the more modern notion that 'the Church makes the Eucharist'.

The relationship between Church and sacraments and the sacramentality of the Church have of course been matters of deep controversy over several centuries. One thing however seems incontrovertible, namely that according to the New Testament Jesus both preached the kingdom of God and never preached it as an abstraction. He never spoke of 'kingdom values', but of the reign of God. And he seems to have expected that those who received his message would live in a new way in relation to other people as well as to the heavenly Father who is both his and theirs.

The old jibe that 'Jesus preached the kingdom of God and what we got was the Catholic Church' is truer (and more necessarily true) than cynics allow. That Christian faith and its institutions are susceptible to distortion appears inevitable given the incarnation of the Word of God and continuation of the Church through history.

It is part of the mystery of Christian faith that ambiguity is always there. As Rowan Williams once wrote, 'By affirming that all "meaning", every assertion about the significance of life and reality, must be judged by reference to a brief succession of contingent events in Palestine, Christianity – almost without realizing it – closed off the path to "timeless truth."'[1]

It follows that the Church may often get it wrong, but it is all we have and its very frailty is a constant challenge to faithfulness.

The capacity for the Church while 'in the world' to tend to become 'of the world' was clearly enhanced as the Church first came to feel itself at home in the world and subsequently became the indispensable ally of the earthly 'powers-that-be'. It may however be significant that in the fourth and fifth centuries a number of the greatest, most learned and holiest priests, monks and theologians were reluctant or even refused to accept a call to the episcopate precisely because this would involve them in public affairs and in the maintenance of the Church as institution and in the defence of its property and other rights in society.

The divisions within Christendom have further encouraged tendencies for 'church leaders' (even this fashionable term is illuminating) to be seen primarily as senior functionaries within organizations. The pastoral and theological seriousness of the consequences of this development cannot be overestimated, although it is not my brief in this short reflection to explore this further.

I intend rather to suggest a few basic principles, the most basic of which is that bishops exist to be expressions of God's own direct care for his people. If Jesus is the final fulfilment of Ezekiel's prophecy, bishops and other ministers must needs be signs of that, at least if they are to continue to be in any recognizable sense 'Christian'.

Anglicans, or at least most of them, have in common with the early and medieval Church and with other historic churches today laid claim to an 'apostolic succession' in ministry, by which they mean an intentional and in principle historically verifiable tradition of bishops from the institution of the apostles. The 'apostolic' nature of the episcopate has however acquired a particular 'slant' in Anglican apologetic. The truth of the doctrine has some-times been obscured by the perceived Anglican need to defend Anglicanism against both the attacks of Rome and the ecclesial claims of more radical Reformation churches. A negative conse-quence of this has sometimes been a tendency to dwell on the institutional continuity of the office and office holders without sufficient anchoring in either doctrine or the wider life of the Catholic Church.

It is important for Anglicans to reclaim a richer understanding of the apostolicity of the Church and its ministry and of the rela-tion of Anglican institutions to it.

This richer understanding was hinted at in the much-neglected *Virginia Report*, which asserted of the bishop's ministry:

> The calling of a bishop is to represent Christ and his Church, par-ticularly as apostle, chief priest, teacher and pastor of a diocese; to guard the faith, unity and discipline of the whole Church; to proclaim the word of God; to act in Christ's name for the rec-onciliation of the world and the building up of the Church; and to ordain others to continue Christ's ministry. (3.17)

It might be wished that the bishop's central role in baptism, confirmation and the Eucharist were more explicit, and it seems strange there is no mention of intercession. Nonetheless, the statement is welcome as far as it goes, and for the purposes of this essay particularly to be noted is the reference to unity and the direct linking of unity with the faith and discipline 'of the whole Church'. Elsewhere in the Report attention is given to the ques-tion of collegiality between bishops and, for Anglicans, the role of the Archbishop of Canterbury and a desire to embed the par-ticipation of all the faithful in the governance of the Church.

The unity of the Anglican Communion and the call to the full visible unity of all the baptized disciples of Jesus – the whole Church – are explicitly linked to the need for human unity. The New Testament vision of all things drawn together into unity with Jesus Christ as Head lies at the heart of the gospel procla-mation and therefore also at the heart of the bishop's ministry.

The service of unity is thus a central feature of the ministry of bishops, and this is of course highlighted in the Ordinals of most Anglican churches.

One reason I regret the lack of explicit mention in the *Virginia Report* of initiation, of the Eucharist and of intercession in relation to the bishop's ministry is that it is precisely these, along with common faith, the proclamation of the Word and a responsibility for discipline, shared with all other bishops, that express the unity of the diocese and that of the diocese with all other local or particular churches.

The apostle's 'care for all the churches' is thus intrinsic to the bishop's office. Of course this is made more difficult, and even impossible, by the fragmented nature of Christianity. There is also a danger that in a divided Church, people imagine that denominational unity is a greater priority than universal unity. Bishops thus become, for example, 'Anglican' bishops, rather than the 'bishops in the Church of God' they were ordained to be. Although in a divided Church this is inevitable, we must never acquiesce in it.

All is not lost, however. Where episcopacy is functioning in a healthy way, bishops (regardless of confessional identity) are often acknowledged even now as exercising a ministry that transcends the boundaries of denomination.

One of the imaginative suggestions in the penultimate agreed statement of ARCIC, *The Gift of Authority*, envisaged the possibility of Anglican bishops joining in *ad limina* visits to Rome with their Roman Catholic counterparts. That the chillier ecumenical climate means that such a notion is currently unlikely does not invalidate the suggestion. Behind it lies an idea that episcopacy might be one of the structures of the 'institution' (in both Tertullian's theological and the more modern sociological sense) whereby there may be a limited anticipation of full visible unity even before all the obstacles to full sacramental communion have been overcome.

It should go without saying that what we are here discussing is not each and every ministry described by the word 'bishop'; nor are we suggesting that only those described by their own communities as 'bishops' share in the Episcopal ministry. The Church, like life, is far more complicated than that. What matters is the identification of God's own care for his people, the seeking by the Good Shepherd for the lost sheep as well as his loving nurture of those who have not strayed.

This short essay is only a starting point for a discussion. I hope however that as Anglicans wrestle with the 'ecclesial deficit' in their Communion, the renewal of the episcopate and understanding of Episcopal ministry may lead them away from denominational isolation into a fuller understanding of what it means to be the Church of Jesus Christ, a shared understanding of which is inseparable from the full sacramental communion of the Church.

Note

1 R. Williams, *The Wound of Knowledge*, London: DLT, 1990, p. 1.

7

THE BISHOP, OTHER CHURCHES, AND GOD'S MISSION 3

C. Christopher Epting

Introduction

When one is made bishop of an Anglican diocese almost anywhere in the world, one finds oneself almost immediately catapulted into the ecumenical arena. There will no doubt be gatherings of 'judicatory leaders' from the various Christian communions on a regular basis. A seat is probably provided for the Anglican bishop on the governing board of the state or regional council of churches, and there will be certain ecumenical decisions to be taken involving joint worship or clergy deployment which can be made by the bishop alone.

This is only as it should be for, in many ways, the bishop is the chief ecumenical officer of his or her diocese. Most Anglican Ordinals contain a vow in which the bishop promises to guard 'the faith, unity, and discipline' of the Church. And surely 'Church' in this context has ecumenical implications. So, at the 2008 Lambeth Conference of bishops, an entire section was devoted to a discussion of 'the bishop, other churches, and God's mission'.

In fact, the focus question for the discussion (*indaba*) groups on Friday 25 July 2008 was 'Working specifically with other churches, how can you as a bishop further the mission we share together in the world?' I want to ground that question theologically by referring to a number of background documents provided for the bishops in a collection simply entitled 'Lambeth Reader' (hereafter referred to as 'LR').

The Anglican Way

In *The Anglican Way: Signposts on a Common Journey*, a paper from the work of a group concerned with Theological Education in the Anglican Communion (TEAC), we read, 'As Anglicans, baptized into Christ, we share in the mission of God with all Christians and are deeply committed to building ecumenical relationships. Our reformed catholic tradition has proved to be a gift we are able to bring to ecumenical endeavor. We invest in dialogue with other churches based on trust and a desire that the whole company of God's people may grow into the fullness of unity to which God calls us that the world may believe the gospel' (LR p. 11). Indeed ecumenism is 'all about mission' carried out in obedience to Jesus' prayer in John 17 that his disciples be one so that the world may believe.

The Inter-Anglican Theological and Doctrinal Commission also contributed an October 2007 paper entitled *The Anglican Way: The Significance of the Episcopal Office for the Communion of the Church*. Here the important point is made that 'bishops of the Anglican Communion have primary responsibility for Anglicans. However, the nature of the Episcopal office means that bishops are called to lead the Church toward deeper *koinonia* among all God's people, and in so doing represent the wider Christian community to the diocese. This universal and ecumenical ministry belongs to the bishop's role as a symbol of unity. Yet this symbol is ambiguous because the Church is divided and torn. In this context the bishop is a sign of a broken Church looking to its Lord for healing and hope through the power of the Spirit' (LR p. 13).

Ecumenism in practice

'The Ministry of Bishops in an Ecumenical Perspective' was included in the 'Lambeth Reader'. It was produced by yet another standing commission of the Anglican Communion, the International Anglican Standing Commission on Ecumenical Relations (IASCER). It begins, 'Anglican bishops today, like bishops of other Churches, exercise their ministry in an ecumenical context. The Anglican theology and practice of Episcopal ministry is grounded in Scripture, finds its classic expression in the patristic period, its traditional expression in Anglican formularies of ordination, and its contemporary expression in Anglican ecumenical agreement. Our ecumenical agreements with other Churches have an important contribution to make to the theology and practice of Episcopal ministry' (LR p. 17). So here, the bishop's very role continues to be defined and shaped by ecumenical agreements between the churches.

This reality was acknowledged more than 20 years ago in 'The Ministry of Bishops' in *The Report of the Lambeth Conference 1988*. In an extract from the section report on mission and ministry we find that 'the holder of the office of bishop needs to work corporately within the total Church in a number of ways: with the laity, deacons, priests and other bishops (if applicable) of the diocese; with the bishops of other dioceses with whom the bishop is "in communion"; with other Christian Churches with whom some degree of communion exists' (LR p. 25). Again, the ecumenical dimension of the bishop's ministry is emphasized in the service of God's mission.

This ecumenical aspect must be highlighted even in the selection, training, and ongoing formation of new bishops if its missional potential is to be realized. The aforementioned 'Theological Education in the Anglican Communion' group (TEAC) produced a series of 'grids' which aim to set out in an accessible way various 'competencies' the group believes are essential for people engaged in various forms of ministry. The Bishops' Target Group believes that even at the nomination or election as a bishop the following quality should be apparent: 'The candidate is alert to ecumenical and inter-faith issues as they may affect the diocese and as these arise in the global context. With training between election or nomination and consecration, or up to the first year as bishop, the following should be evident . . . the new bishop encourages honest and open ecumenical and inter-faith relationship. [And] during tenure of office for all bishops . . . the bishop ensures that targeted training is provided for key diocesan personnel' (LR p. 32). This last reminds us that the bishop does not carry out his or her ecumenical ministry alone but should foster a network of support for this work, including appointing an ecumenical officer for the diocese and possibly establishing ecumenical and inter-faith commissions to raise visibility and support.

Ecumenism in new agreed statements

Two new 'agreed statements' from ecumenical partners were introduced to the bishops at the 2008 Lambeth Conference: *Growing Together in Unity and Mission: An Agreed Statement of the International Anglican–Roman Catholic Commission for Unity and Mission* and *The Church of the Triune God: The Cyprus Agreed Statement of the International Commission for Anglican –Orthodox Theological Dialogue*. Summaries of these watershed statements were included in the 'Lambeth Reader' as examples of the fruit of patient ecumenical dialogue over many years.

Growing Together in Unity and Mission is in fact a document written by bishops for bishops (of both communions). Part One 'treats nine areas where Anglicans and Roman Catholics share a high degree of agreement in faith. Their understanding of: God as Trinity; the Church as communion in mission; the Word of God; baptism; Eucharist; ministry; authority in the Church; discipleship and holiness; and the Blessed Virgin Mary. But Part One also points clearly to a number of areas where differences exist between Anglicans and Roman Catholics' (LR p. 59).

Even with such disagreements remaining 'the bishops go on to invite Anglicans and Roman Catholics to consider what practical suggestions for joint action in mission are appropriate to their particular context . . . The practical suggestions [include] . . . visible expressions of our shared faith; joint study of our faith; cooperation in ministry; and shared witness in the world' (LR pp. 59–60).

In more detail, these suggestions include: joint baptismal preparation; the renewal of baptismal promise together; attending each other's Eucharist (respecting the differing disciplines on receiving Communion); pilgrimages; the saying together of the daily office; joint Bible study and the study of ecumenical texts together; bishops meeting together and attending each other's collegial and synodical gatherings; shared mission to promote social justice; to eradicate poverty; and to care for the environment (LR p. 60). There is much to be done together in mission already in our 'real but imperfect communion' as Anglicans and Roman Catholics. What is preventing it?

Some would argue that divisive issues within Anglicanism and within other churches as well have distracted us from our ecumenical vocation and slowed the pace of the progress toward full, visible unity for which we once hoped. Yet we are reminded in the Anglican–Orthodox statement, *The Church of the Triune God*, that 'the ecumenical journey of our two churches is bringing them new insights and bearing fruit, and is indeed vital for them. Searching questions about the eschatological, Christological, and local character of the Church require a fresh assessment of current patterns of ecclesial life. Mutual questioning in charity and ecclesial fellowship reveals aspects of church life which may need to be changed. Since each church is facing issues including those of unity and diversity, and orthodoxy and dissent, this process may open up new horizons, and we may be able to help each other more than we can imagine' (LR p. 65).

Even in the bishops' discussion of the St Andrew's Draft of a proposed 'Anglican Covenant' designed to reduce some of the tensions within the Anglican Communion, the ecumenical dimension is not absent. In Section I.1.6 of the draft document each church of the Communion would be asked to affirm 'that it participates in the apostolic mission of the whole people of God, and that this mission is shared with other Churches and traditions beyond this Covenant', and in 11.1.3 that 'we embrace opportunities for the discovery of the life of the whole gospel and for reconciliation and shared mission with the Church throughout the world. It is with all the saints that we will comprehend the fuller dimensions of Christ's redemptive and immeasurable love' (LR pp. 80–1).

What does it all mean?

And is not that the point really? Anglicans have never claimed that we are 'the true Church'. There is a certain 'provisionality' in Anglicanism which is seen, not as a weakness, but as a potential strength. We know that we need others, and to be in communion with others, in order to 'comprehend the fuller dimensions of Christ's redemptive and immeasurable love'.

In fact, each expression of the tragically shattered body of Christ has preserved, perhaps even held in trust, some important aspect of the Church Catholic. One might mention Roman Catholic universality, Orthodox spirituality, Anglican liturgy, Lutheran theological precision, Methodist social consciousness, Reformed preaching, Baptist zeal for evangelism, and other such treasures. The Church will never live up to her potential as a witness to her Lord until these qualities are once again reunited in full, visible unity which the world can recognize.

Bishops have a particular responsibility and role to play in this search for unity. The 'Preface to the Ordination Rites' in the 1979 American *Book of Common Prayer* begins: 'The Holy Scriptures and ancient Christian writers make it clear that from the apostles' time, there have been different ministries within the Church. In particular, since the time of the New Testament, three distinct orders or ordained ministers have been characteristic of Christ's holy catholic Church. First, there is the order of bishops who carry on the apostolic work of leading, supervising, and uniting the Church' (p. 510). The text continues with equally succinct definitions of the ministries of presbyters and deacons.

But our focus here is on the ministry of 'the bishop, other churches, and God's mission'. And the Preface's definition of the bishop's 'apostolic work' is useful here – leading, supervising, and uniting the Church. First of all, the bishop must lead. Whether in the local diocese or the national church, if bishops do not take the lead in initiating, supporting, and encouraging ecumenical dialogue and cooperation, it will not happen. As the Presiding Bishop's Deputy for Ecumenical and Inter-religious Relations in The Episcopal Church, the author could point you to numerous examples – both positively and negatively – of the effect of Episcopal leadership (or lack of it) on the ecumenical movement.

Second, the bishop 'supervises'. This is a fair English translation of the Greek *episcopos* or overseer. By virtue of his or her particular vocation and ministry, a bishop is privileged to glimpse 'the big picture' whether in diocese, national church, the wider Communion, or indeed the universal Church. It has been said that 'God's Church doesn't have a mission . . . rather God's mission has a Church'. But if the Church is called and gifted to participate in God's mission of reconciliation we must also recognize that this vocation is too challenging for a divided Church. How will the world ever believe in the One whom God has sent if our very gospel is proclaimed in such divergent, and even conflicting, ways by the various Christian 'communions?' A clear, cogent, and coherent witness is needed in our increasingly secular and 'post-Christian' age.

Which should lead us to the third characteristic of Episcopal ministry – the bishop 'unites the Church'. Not alone certainly for it is the work of God's Holy Spirit to unify the Church. But time and time again we heard at the Lambeth Conference of the bishop's role as 'symbol of unity', uniting congregations into a diocese, dioceses into a national church, the national church into the worldwide Communion, and, yes, the Anglican Communion into the one, holy, catholic, and apostolic Church of the creeds.

We do not do this perfectly. And here it is good to be reminded of this poignant sentence from *The Anglican Way: The Significance of the Episcopal Office for the Communion of the Church* cited above: '. . . this symbol [of unity] is ambiguous because the Church is divided and torn. In this context the bishop is a sign of a broken Church looking to its Lord for healing and hope through the power of the Spirit.' This is our challenge as Anglican bishops today. Pray God that we shall be up to it.

8

ENGAGING WITH A MULTI-FAITH WORLD 1

Suheil S. Dawani

Theological reflection on the relationship of Christians with members of other faiths is a large part of our ministry here in the Diocese of Jerusalem. Our clergy and people, our teachers and students, our doctors, nurses and patients live, by definition, in a multi-faith world. For us, this is neither an academic exercise nor a topic of theological conversation after dinner. We are engaged all the time in the realities of multi-faith relationships. We are blessed by God in the challenges and blessings which these relationships provide for our ministry.

As students of the Bible we know how important it is to grasp the context of the passage we are reading. We gain a better understanding of the words on the page when we understand something about the author, the surroundings and the way of life of the people whose story we read. We are better able to grasp something of God's intent when we are more fully informed of the context of the life of the people of God and in so doing we learn from their relationship with one another and their relationship with God.

So it is for the Christian community which still exists in the Land of the Holy One. The context of our ministry as the Episcopal Diocese of Jerusalem is multi-faith, multi-national and multicultural. Our context includes relationships with Jews, Muslims and a variety of Christian traditions spread out over five countries which include Israel, the Palestinian National Authority, Lebanon, Syria, Jordan plus Jerusalem and Gaza. Before we can grapple with issues and opportunities of this multifaith environment, we benefit from a deeper understanding of the Christian community which claims its identity in the first Pentecost.

Palestinian Christians represented approximately 23 per cent of the total Arab population of pre-1948 Palestine. Today this same population represents less than 2 per cent of the total and faces possible extinction in the near future. Even when we add all the Christians together from the Orthodox, Latin and Reformed traditions, we are very much a minority community throughout the region. The rate of decline is most notable in Jerusalem and the West Bank. The so-called 'out migration' of many Christian families is largely the result of social and economic pressures made worse by the ongoing regional conflicts which plague our area. Recent research informs us that these same regional conflicts create a climate of religious and cultural intolerance which only adds to the economic pressures to leave. This same research tells us that our people are interested in staying in the Holy Land if they are able to enjoy an adequate standard of living with some sense of job security. However, the combination of social and economic factors encourages many of our young people to take their talent and their hope for the future elsewhere.

Historically, the Christians of the Land of the Holy One are the descendants of those who were here for the first Pentecost. We have been and continue to be an integral part of Palestinian society. Christians welcome the opportunity to take our place in the leadership of initiatives to improve the lives of our people and our neighbours. Christians, more exposed to western culture and education, have always been considered major contributors in our society and provide leadership and expertise in crucial educational and health services, without discrimination of any kind. Christians have also played very important leadership roles in the politics of our region and in the various public and private sectors of the economy.

By virtue of the presence and active participation of Christians throughout this region, it is well recognized that the education and values of local Christians help to create respectful and constructive dialogue among people of different faiths, economic circumstances and cultural traditions. As a consequence, the urgency to preserve an indigenous Christian community in the Holy Land and the Middle East is as crucial as the need for Christians to continue to serve as a moderating element in the social, cultural and spiritual fabric of the Middle East.

While other communities of faith do exist within our diocese, our major points of contact are obviously with the Muslim and Jewish communities. Our presence as a minority faith community within a larger Muslim population throughout most of our diocese and a larger Jewish population within the nation of Israel provides remarkable challenges and opportunities for constructive engagement with both Islam and Judaism.

With the end of the British Mandate in 1948 and the establishment of the nation of Israel, the Diocese of Jerusalem 'inherited' schools, hospitals and rehabilitation centres serving those with a wide variety of needs in terms of education, health care and other services to improve their quality of life. Currently we sponsor 19 schools and rehabilitation/educational programmes ranging from kindergartens to full programmes from pre-school to secondary school. Our schools are highly respected for the education provided by professional and compassionate teachers and administrators with high standards.

The education of the young people of the Holy Land is a high priority for us and provides vital contact and communication with our neighbours in the towns, villages and cities which we serve. Most of our students are Muslim. In some of our schools the total Muslim student body exceeds 95 per cent. The students, faculty, administration and support staffs are fully integrated to include both Christians and Muslims.

Education is a key element in encouraging Christian families, among others, to remain in the Holy Land. Having good schools available is important to young families. Good education always requires financial support. We find in our diocese that this is especially true in Jerusalem and throughout the West Bank where there is a need to improve school facilities, train teachers and assist with tuition fees for families of more than two children.

We also see a need for scholarship assistance in higher education to enable local youth to remain in the region instead of going elsewhere for their university training. Some of our most talented students are offered full scholarships at a variety of foreign colleges and universities. On the one hand this is a great testimony to the education we provide our young people, while on the other hand we find those same talented young people often stay in the country of their university education. By providing scholarship assistance for these students to attend university in the region, we may be able to encourage them to stay here after graduation to provide a valuable skilled resource for a stable Palestinian economy and social infrastructure. Retaining an educated population is critical to the future of our region.

Our schools provide and teach Christian values of love, respect and equality for all people. This message of tolerance and moderation is a key contribution of the Christian community and, I believe, is a vital effort for promoting peace for all of God's people. We take seriously our role in educating the next generation of peace-makers.

The social and political context in which the Christian community exists here in the Holy Land requires us to live in close contact with others whose theological perspectives are quite different from ours. Our willingness to embrace our neighbours as full members of society and as citizens who work for the good of all of God's people, and their willingness to live in harmony with us, creates close bonds of affection and cooperation.

This is critically important to emphasize. Many media outlets continue to stress division and enmity among the three so-called Abrahamic Faiths. Too often only the most sensational and negative comments get on the air or appear in the print media. While it is true that acts of violence do take place between radical groups from time to time, let us understand that many other social, economic, political and historical factors play a role in such random acts of violence. Too often such acts are much less about individuals who hold to a certain faith, but rather the frustration and anger of the perpetrator against what they think the 'church', 'synagogue' or 'mosque' represents. We must seek to look behind the stories in the news to more fully grasp the meaning of a brief news video or article.

Without romanticizing these tensions, we might ask, if relations among the three faiths with which we work the most were dangerous, how could our diocese employ so many hundreds of staff from these various faith traditions for our hospitals, schools and rehabilitation centres? If mutual respect was not present for the students and faculties of our schools, how could we provide a safe educational environment for these same students from these traditions?

The root of this positive engagement with Muslim and Jewish families throughout our diocese has to do with a willingness to shed what divides us and embrace what unites us. The term 'Abrahamic Faiths' is often used to describe the common link between Jews, Christians and Muslims. While Abraham is revered by us all, there is more to our relationship in faith than this important person.

Our engagement with the multi-faith world in which we live has everything to do with mutual respect and a deep desire to raise up the values we share which are common to the Christian, Jewish and Muslim communities. Our ministry is entirely about a 'ministry of presence' in the villages, towns and cities where our churches, hospitals, schools and clinics exist. In the same way in which our Lord Jesus Christ was fully present with those who were in need and whose lives he touched, we continue that same presence throughout this diocese.

Our engagement with our multi-faith environment mirrors the compassionate love of our Lord for all people. We provide clinics and schools to assist children and adults who are low-vision and those who are blind; the hard of hearing and the deaf; the mentally challenged and those who are confined to wheelchairs. We provide job-training and rehabilitation services for all of these people among our neighbours without regard to their ability to pay for these services and without regard to their religion. The compassion of God knows no boundary of race, creed, culture or language.

The engagement we find most useful is found neither in converting members of other faiths to the way we understand God nor in convincing others to join the Church through the rites and sacraments of the Christian tradition. We engage others by the witness of our example in our way of life which is one of respect and understanding.

There is a significant amount of unfortunate history for both the Jewish and Muslim communities in relation to the triumphalism and imperialism which some segments of the Christian community have perpetrated upon Jews and Muslims over the centuries. I need not go into great detail on this, but a few words will remind you of that history: Inquisition; Crusades; pogroms; Holocaust; fundamentalism. For the Palestinian community, there is also the *Nakba* (Catastrophe) of 1948, when thousands of Muslim and Christian Palestinians were removed from their lands and villages during Israel's War of Independence.

Each of these words brings up emotions among many of us which we need to recognize and accept. The impact of the history of relationships which have arisen in various centuries, some recent and some ongoing, between the Abrahamic Faiths is very real among many people of these communities. While this is true, we must also recognize that the images which come to mind from these words of history also run against our understanding of the values which will build up relationships of mutual respect, understanding and tolerance.

We cannot allow the past errors of judgement in word and action to be repeated. We must be informed by the past but not shackled by it. We must remember the times in the past and recognize the circumstances in the present in which generosity and forbearance between the faiths has existed and we must build on those examples of good-will and mutual respect. We cannot allow future action to be dictated by fear and hopelessness rooted in the sordid stories of those in each faith who have led their people astray. As a consequence, a large part of our engagement with our Abrahamic brothers and sisters is focused on developing trust between all parties.

What better way to develop such trust than through the education of the next generation of peace-makers even as we heal the current generation of those in need of medical care? We overcome the past by not repeating the mistakes of that past (or dwelling upon them) and by encouraging new opportunities for dialogue within the bounds of relationships which promote mutual respect.

In *An Open Letter and Call from Muslim Religious Leaders* to His Holiness Pope Benedict XVI and Heads of Churches throughout Christendom dated 13 October 2007, we find the foundation of the shared values which promote a deep level of commitment and communication for the Abrahamic faith community. The love of God and our neighbour is at the heart of who we are as Christians, Muslims and Jews:

> Whilst Islam and Christianity are obviously different religions – and whilst there is no minimising some of their formal differences – it is clear that the *Two Greatest Commandments* are an area of common ground and a link between the Qur'an, the Torah and the New Testament. What prefaces the Two Commandments in the Torah and the New Testament, and what they arise out of, is the Unity of God – that there is only one God. For the *Shema* in the Torah starts: 'Hear, O Israel: The LORD our God, the LORD is one!' (Deuteronomy 6:4) Likewise, Jesus said: 'The first of all the commandments is: "Hear, O Israel, the LORD our God, the LORD is one."' (Mark 12:29) Likewise, God says in the Holy Qur'an: 'Say: He, God, is One. God, the Self-Sufficient Besought of all' (*Al-Ikhlas*, 112:1–2). Thus the Unity of God, love of Him, and love of the neighbour form a common ground upon which Islam and Christianity (and Judaism) are founded.
>
> This could not be otherwise since Jesus said: 'On these two commandments hang all the Law and the Prophets.' (Matthew 22:40) Moreover, God confirms in the Holy Qur'an that the Prophet Muhammad brought nothing fundamentally or essentially new: 'Naught is said to thee (Muhammad) but what already was said to the messengers before thee' (*Fussilat* 41:43).

And: 'Say (Muhammad): I am no new thing among the messengers (of God), nor know I what will be done with me or with you. I do but follow that which is Revealed to me, and I am but a plain warner' (*Al-Ahqaf*, 46:9). Thus also God in the Holy Qur'an confirms that the same eternal truths of the Unity of God, of the necessity for total love and devotion to God (and thus shunning false gods), and of the necessity for love of fellow human beings (and thus justice), underlie all true religion.

The values we share with our Muslim and Jewish brothers and sisters are a focus on God, a love for our neighbour and a willingness to live with the differences we have. These are the values which are required for us to enjoy the life which God has given us to share in the Holy Land. Without these values put to work in word and deed, the peace of God which passes all understanding will have no room to grow for us, and indeed for the whole world. These are the values which we share every day through our ministry of presence and service in our hospitals, schools, rehabilitation centres and through our parishes.

Our engagement in this multi-faith effort for peace and reconciliation, rooted in love of God and love of neighbour, is at the heart of inter-faith dialogue. Here in Jerusalem we have 13 Christian churches recognized by the government of Israel, each of which actively participates in both ecumenical and inter-faith dialogues to promote better understanding and to assist in setting an example of active reconciliation efforts. Such cooperation is vital. The Heads of Churches in Jerusalem have been active in inter-faith dialogue with our Jewish and Muslim communities and leaders and continue to meet on a monthly basis. In this way, the Heads of Churches are paving the way toward improved understanding and respect, and peace and reconciliation between all people of the Holy City which we pray has a positive impact throughout the religious communities we represent.

Inviting, developing and nurturing relationships is the key to our engagement with our multi-faith context for ministry. Hospitality in our culture is a way of life. Arabs embrace the opportunity to visit with one another and welcome others to join for coffee or tea to discuss the issues of the day. This hospitality means more than good manners or simple kindness. Through fostering such relationships we find opportunity for discussion of the most important issues which confront our people, our families and the world in which we live. To be sure, not every conversation over coffee yields deep insight, but among Arab Muslims and Arab Christians there is a shared cultural desire for relationships in which to share life's joys and sorrows as well as a yearning to grasp a sense of God's will for our lives.

In the Diocese of Jerusalem, throughout the five countries we serve, it is this shared culture which provides some common ground for the building and nurturing of relationships. In our schools, it is through relationships forged with our students and their parents, our faculties and administrators which promotes healthy relationships in a new generation of those who have different faiths. In our hospitals, clinics and rehabilitation centres, it is through the privileged relationships between our doctors and their patients as well as between our nurses and their patients that we engage at the deepest levels the needs of God's people, Christian, Jewish and Muslim alike.

People of faith have a deep reverence for the concept which surrounds the word 'covenant'. We understand covenant to be something much more than a legal agreement. I so appreciate the words of Rabbi Sir Jonathan Sacks, Chief Rabbi for the United Hebrew Congregations of the Commonwealth, when he addressed the Lambeth Conference in July of 2008. Rabbi Sacks said:

In a covenant, two or more individuals, each respecting the dignity and the integrity of the other, come together in a bond of love and trust, to share their interests, sometimes even to share their lives, by pledging our faithfulness to one another, to do together what neither of us can do alone.

And that is not the same as a contract at all. A contract is a *transaction*, but a covenant is a *relationship*. Or to put it slightly differently: a contract is about interests, but a covenant is about identity. And that is why contracts *benefit*, but covenants *transform*. [emphasis his]

Engagement for the Christian community of my diocese is about the transformation of relationships from suspicion to trust, from extremism to moderation, from fundamentalism to toleration and from despair to hope. We focus our ministry on developing relationships which allow covenants of trust and hope to grow and develop for the benefit of all the people of the Holy Land and to inspire all of God's creation to seek relationships of reconciliation and peace.

As Christians we are rooted in our love of God and love of our neighbour to continue to play an important role in building bridges of dialogue, peace and understanding between East and West and between Christianity, Judaism and Islam. These bridges are vital for the dignity and security of all people in this region and for peace in all of God's creation. Engagement with a multi-faith world is entirely what the Christian community in the Land of the Holy One is all about.

May God bless us and keep us.

Amen.

9

ENGAGING WITH A MULTI-FAITH WORLD 2

Michael Jackson

Introduction

Lambeth 2008 was my first opportunity to attend and participate in a Lambeth Conference, as I was consecrated bishop in 2002 to serve in a rural diocese in Ireland. For most of my episcopate to date, there has been sustained speculation about whether Lambeth 2008 was going to happen at all; who was going to be invited; who was going to come or who was going to stay away. In the end, approximately 660 bishops attended, making up three quarters of the current complement of bishops in the Anglican Communion. Although Lambeth 2008 was diminished by the absence of more than 200 fellow bishops, there was no sense that it was depressed or defeated in carrying out the work which lay before it. We came from the worlds in which we work and to them we have returned. During July and August 2008 we shared something of those worlds with one another.

It is quite a challenge to reprogramme 660 people who are accustomed to taking a lead and being listened to! By reprogramming I mean enabling them to be open to the Spirit of God and to one another. You might well say: why was it necessary to spend two and a half weeks and approaching eight million dollars to do this for people who are tremendously privileged and ought already to be doing this for themselves and also doing it for others? You might also say: with the ease of modern methods of communication could all of this not, in any case, have been done by email and web-based material? I answer: people still need to meet and become friends in Christ.

All of us know how rapid the pace of change is in today's world. Technology and swift communications combine with a popularized philosophy of postmodernism to create insecurities about received wisdom and to foster the need for new certainties to which people can hold fast. This is happening because people sense that it seems as if the pace of change is always being forced by someone *else*. The Anglican Communion and the office of bishop have been affected by this every bit as much as anyone or anything else. In order to create and sustain human, personal understanding beyond website caricatures of people and positions, Lambeth 2008 offered to every bishop in the Anglican Communion who was granted an invitation by the Archbishop of Canterbury the opportunity to have her or his voice heard – but also to meet other bishops.

The purpose of Lambeth 2008

This purposeful meeting was twofold in intention: to explore Anglican identity and to equip bishops for mission as bishops of the whole Church and as bishops of their particular diocese. It was also an opportunity to interact with Ecumenical Partners in a way which enriched the range and the depth of discussion. Those who planned the Conference did so with particular aims in mind to facilitate a range of different types of listening and speaking at a variety of levels. The retreat in Canterbury Cathedral, where the Archbishop of Canterbury gave each address, prepared the ground in a particular way; in listening both to the archbishop and to the silence, bishops were being prepared to listen both to God and neighbour.

There were other opportunities to talk and to listen. The Windsor Continuation Group and the Covenant Design Group were, clearly in retrospect, the engine-rooms of the Conference. They were designed to get us to where the organizers wanted to help us to get. Both had come to birth and life out of the crisis in the Communion originating in the Episcopal consecration of Gene Robinson. Both, however, have subsequently developed a life and a debate of their own in the Anglican world and they drew large numbers of people who wanted to have their say on a wide range of issues, themselves relating to the underlying matters of human sexuality, authority and obedience – and communion itself. Throughout these Hearings there was a level of respect and attentiveness which few expected to be sustained – but it was!

The *indaba* process seems to be where the hopes for a new form of personal engagement by bishops with bishops lay. *Indaba* is a Zulu concept, a gathering for purposeful discussion, a particular method and process of engagement. It presupposes a willingness to meet and converse about seriously divisive issues as well as ensuring voices are not suppressed. Under the guidance of the Holy Spirit, deeper convergences were sought which might hold people together in difference along with reaching a deeper understanding of issues discussed. To anyone who has kept abreast of developments and difficulties in the Communion, *indaba* provided the bishops at Lambeth with opportunity to go together behind superficialities and, in communion, to test the old maxim: what unites is ultimately more important than what divides.

Equipping bishops for mission

Along with the retreat in Canterbury Cathedral, regular daily worship, and Bible study of St John's Gospel – itself very conscious of Christianity's being placed in a context both of derivation from and active hostility from another World Faith – the *indabas* covered the following areas, asking of bishops that they share from their own place and experience and learn from one another.

The *indaba* areas were: Mission and Evangelism; Human and Social Justice; Environment; Ecumenism; Relations with other

World Religions; Anglican Bishops; Anglican Identity; Human Sexuality; The Scriptures; The Anglican Covenant (St Andrew's Draft); The Windsor Process.

For the 'Relations with other World Religions' *indaba*, NIFCON prepared a DVD incorporating snapshots of inter-faith activity and reflection by bishops, present at the Lambeth Conference, in the following areas of the world: Egypt, Pakistan, Sri Lanka, Sudan, Canada and England. This gave a broad spread of Episcopal and ecclesiastical experience on the ground and was complemented by an erudite yet thoroughly accessible discussion of the theological issues involved in inter-faith encounter by Mrs Clare Amos and Archdeacon Michael Ipgrave, both experienced members of the NIFCON Management Group. It was fortunate that the inter-faith *indaba* took place just before the tempo and temperature changed with the emphasis shifting to Human Sexuality.

Generous love

The document *Generous Love: The truth of the Gospel and the call to dialogue* came into being through a NIFCON initiative to provide a theology of inter-faith relations as a piece of self-consciously Anglican theological writing. This project readily received the support of the Archbishop of Canterbury. Lambeth 1988 and Lambeth 1998 were both seriously concerned with inter-faith issues and encounter as being part of the weave of Anglican identity and Anglican expression. Thus *Generous Love* speaks constructively into the experience – often one of dilemma and bewilderment – which many bishops, clergy and people feel in the face of an inter-faith reality which is a human reality of neighbours.

The shape of *Generous Love* is as follows:

1. Beginning with God
2. Our contemporary context and our Anglican heritage
3. Shaping Anglican insights: reading the Scriptures

4. Shaping Anglican insights: tradition and reason
5. Celebrating the presence of Christ's body
6. Communicating the energy of the Spirit
7. Practising the embassy and hospitality of God
8. Sending and abiding.

Generous Love speaks of those essential Christ-like acts and deeds of love being generous in three main pairs: presence and engagement; embassy and hospitality; sending and abiding.

These provide the tent-pegs for the journey of discovery or pilgrimage of disclosure of God which lies at the heart of inter-faith encounter. They also seek to root and ground in real experience what it is like to live both at the edge (of encounter with others) and at the centre (of encounter with Jesus Christ).

Generous Love is neither a theology of religions nor, again, a systematic theology. It is, primarily, a theological perspective from within the Anglican tradition on the sort of inter-faith work and witness which Anglicans everywhere are called and invited to do as Christian people in everyday life. Many people have strong and strongly differing perspectives on the role of Christians in today's world. *Generous Love*, however, seeks to give voice to the twin perspectives of mission and strengthening identity – concepts pivotal to the Retreat Addresses given to the Lambeth Conference 2008 by the Archbishop of Canterbury. *Generous Love* significantly widens the remit beyond the confines of bishops *per se* to include the lay people and the clergy of the Anglican Communion in their local setting. It is for this reason that *Generous Love* is for the Communion at large and therefore it is given to all Anglicans whether present at Lambeth or not.

Generous love – its broadest sweep

One of the most interesting things was that the Archbishop of Canterbury himself took up the words *generous love* in his final address to the bishops. This is significant in that, at the point at which the continuance of communion was at its most important, in the minds and on the hearts of Lambeth participants, when bishops present were listening to their host at Canterbury, *generous love* was offered, with conscious literary allusion and theological imperative, as a method of gracious engagement within and across the Anglican Communion itself. This has inspired me, under the encouragement of Mrs Clare Amos, Director of Theological Studies in the Anglican Communion, to offer you a reading of the Lambeth Conference 2008 itself through the lens of *Generous Love*. To this end I offer a selection of themes but an overview of experience.

Generous love – snapshots of its themes in the light of Canterbury

1. Beginning with God

Lambeth 2008, for the first time at a Lambeth Conference, began in retreat. Bishops were encouraged to seize the moment, to take hold of the space – Canterbury Cathedral and its precincts were set aside for two days exclusively for the use of bishops attending. During this time, bishops were asked simply to listen to God, to silence, to one another and to the Archbishop of Canterbury. The archbishop encouraged fellow bishops to think about what it meant to be a person in whom God reveals Jesus, particularly revealing the Jesus who gathers. The archbishop's argument was that for a bishop to be a sign of unity, that bishop must model and elicit mutual self-giving in order to enable the community to assemble (*ekklesia*) to reveal Jesus both within and beyond itself.

Looking, with such a perspective, to *Generous Love* we see the vastness of God in the face of the delusions of a human knowledge which fails to acknowledge its limitations; the person of Jesus in life, death, resurrection as making known the triune reality of God; the sending in mission – significantly a mission of renewal and restoration – of life and love in which we are called

to share, energized today by the Spirit. By our personal participation in the primary sending of the Son of God, we ourselves
are called to be present to and to engage with our neighbours of
faiths other than our own in a manner which is missional and
incarnational. A dynamic Trinitarian self-understanding on the
part of the children of God is modelled and shared in Christ-like
action.

2. Context and Bible

Lambeth 2008 sought to take the contexts from which bishops
came more seriously perhaps than any previous Lambeth. The
thinking behind this was the rapidity of change in today's world
and the disparity of understanding and affection which results
from such change. There is also a widespread paralysis of engagement even though there is a broader experience of knowing.
This is one of the besetting ironies of our contemporary world.
Pivotal to this is the emphasis placed at Lambeth 2008 on Bible
studies and active, participative membership of the Bible study
groups which in turn formed the bedrock of *indaba* groups. Worship and Bible study were neither incidental nor an add-on in
Lambeth 2008. They were a cross-cultural gathering of bishops,
experienced and inexperienced, around the Gospel of John. Bishops not only read and discussed the specific passage for study
daily, but were actively encouraged to relate it in exegesis and
discussion to the progressive themes of the days of the Conference itself and to the *indaba* which followed Bible study each
day. The Bible studies of themselves encouraged bishops together
to reflect on their own individual contexts and those of their
people. In this way, Scripture became a prism through which
were refracted God, the Word of God and the current contexts of
leadership and service in which bishops and Ecumenical Partners
are living out their faith. Furthermore Anglicanism has always
sought to work out its concerns historically, relevant to particular contexts, following the example of the incarnate Christ who
worked in a particular historical context of human life. It was

very clear that Scripture is part of the contemporary context. As well as being a *casus belli* among others in the current difficulties of the Anglican Communion, it is a place where people can meet and be renewed. In this way, Bible and context together took the spirit of the Retreat into the continuum of the Conference.

Generous Love recognizes with chilling realism the importance of context and of recognizing that with migration, either enforced or elective, contexts which once were homogeneous now are marked by diversity of religions. Such migration and the challenges it presents both to the people newly arrived and to the host country are a spin-off of globalization. All of this provides an imperative as well as an opportunity literally to confront – to face-to-face with and not to turn our backs on – our neighbour made in God's image and likeness but not con-formed to our particular Faith. As *Generous Love* voices it: 'In every context, whatever its historical background and current pressures, we face the challenge of discerning the loving purposes of God within the religious plurality of humankind.' *Generous Love* further argues that the experience of Anglicanism through and subsequent to the Reformation continues to inform and equip it for living in a world of diversity, but one which ultimately coheres within the purpose of God the creator and is not an *à la carte* of relativism in word or deed. It states: 'This is a discipline against sectarianism, and a resource for living with plurality.'

3. Anglican identity and insights

Scripture, Tradition and Reason lie at the root of Anglican methodology. As a triadic response to the work of God in the world, we owe their formulation to the late sixteenth-century theologian Richard Hooker. These three strands have proved to be invaluable as a way of hammering out Anglican identity beyond the Established Church of England, as well as within the Church of England of which Hooker was a son. People interpret the inter-relation of these three elements in different ways. What is clear from Hooker is the primacy of Scripture informed by a fundamental principle of natural law whose 'seat is the bosom of God, her voice the harmony of the world' (Hooker: 1.16.8): everything is subservient to such natural law as the expression of God's supreme reason. The response to this is both organic and dynamic since, by analogy from everyday life, the permanence of law does not preclude development in detail. This natural law is, finally, the expression of God's supreme reason. From this pattern of thought derives the dynamic understanding of tradition as the Church interpreting, not the Church reminiscing. This in turn enables the Church of God, through the Anglican Communion, to respond in faith and in courage to what happens in each unfolding generation.

The question of identity was very much to the fore throughout the Lambeth Conference. *Generous Love* addresses this in sections three and four, once again taking further into the Anglican Communion what was lived out by the participants in Lambeth 2008. The document is very clear on the primacy of Scripture with the insights of tradition and reason applied to the text in the light of historical and contemporary experience. Scripture has already 'been there' before us in that both Judaism and Christianity have lived amidst religious plurality, an experience which has shaped the formative texts of both sets of Scriptures. This is both a resource and an impetus when appropriately applied.

Particularly in relation to Scripture, *Generous Love* identifies and explains the fresh voice which is given to Scripture through the practice of 'Scriptural Reasoning', that is, reading the Bible alongside members of other World Faiths who themselves read their Scriptures. Each party does so with utter honesty and the sense each has of being addressed by God through the Scriptures. Tradition and reason likewise are expounded in *Generous Love* in such a way as to give urgency to inter-faith encounter as not being something disloyal to Christianity itself. The *Virginia Report* (1997) indeed holds together Scripture, Tradition and Reason as being quintessentially Anglican in their interaction. As *Generous Love* puts it: 'Anglicans hold that Scripture is to be interpreted in the light of tradition and reason, meaning by these an appeal respectively, to the mind of the Church as that develops and to the mind of the cultures in which the Church participates.' Again we see that the Anglican theological method places and holds Anglicans in every generation in Scripture, Church and Society. These go hand in hand with another triad: prayer and worship; concern for the welfare of the whole of society; the centrality of pastoral practice. In this way Anglican engagement with religious (not simply intra-denominational) difference remains a key testing ground for discipleship and this is worked through on a spectrum between conversion and accommodation within a pro-active definition of mission.

Generous Love extracts from this discussion three doublets: presence and engagement; embassy and hospitality; sending and abiding as paradigms of inter-faith encounter. These three pairs of words are important in implementing locally and in understanding locally what it is to be a Christian oriented on inter-faith encounter and engagement. They are not heady aspirations but descriptions and paradigms of inter-faith life.

All of these pairs of doing things in the name of God which are paradigms of inter-faith encounter were present at Lambeth 2008. One of the most exhilarating expressions of communion and the Communion was the way in which consistently people stuck with it and engaged in it. This was true of early morning worship, evening lectures, the demanding timetable of Bible study, *indaba* and self-select sessions together with the various Hearings as they took root in the lives of Lambeth participants. Hospitality was modelled and offered by the Archbishop of Canterbury and Mrs Williams *par excellence*, both by their friendly and gracious presence on the campus of the University of Kent and by their receptions for episcopal participants and spouses throughout the period of Lambeth. There was a further sense of embassy and hospitality in that, by their various pertinent interventions and summations at specific points, they drew out where the Conference had reached and drew together threads and possible directions of engagement for the subsequent phases. The theme of sending and abiding, itself thoroughly Johannine, likewise pervaded Lambeth 2008. The archbishop's Retreat Addresses, with which proceedings began, are entitled 'God's Mission and the Bishop's Discipleship'.

The invitation to Lambeth provided an opportunity and gave permission for such explorations in trust. We must always remember the power of affectionate authority as well as of moral authority in relation to the Archbishop of Canterbury. The Conference gave participants the opportunity to live a love which is generous in their own person and in new relationships of understanding, respect and cooperation being formed. One of the most significant 'sendings' took place during the Final Service in Canterbury Cathedral. The Melanesians had shaped and sustained our worship and through prayer, chaplaincy, healing and liturgy reformulated our belonging to one another; they also enabled us to be equipped to abide in the risen Christ in a very special way as we left Canterbury. Unforgettable was the vignette of liturgy embedded in the final Eucharist whereby the names of the Melanesian Martyrs of 2003 were laid up in the Cathedral. The community of Melanesian Brothers and Sisters who had sustained us throughout the Conference took the book of the names of those martyrs deeper and deeper into the house of God in which the initial retreat had taken place. As this happened, their Litany of the Saints became more faint to hear but more permanent to the memory. It was a moment when *anamnesis* became a living reality – indeed an abiding which sent us out.

4. Presence and engagement

I select this pair, presence and engagement, in particular to give a flavour of the strength and the vitality, together with some of the difficulties and dangers, of the Anglican involvement with inter-faith situations. The going is often far from easy. Anglicans are present in any inter-faith context primarily through their being there and through engaging with those who along with them form that community. Worship of God, most widely understood, has always been the way in which Anglicans express their identity. Such worship brings with it a sense of sacred space, sacred time and lives consecrated to God for God's hallowing. All of these issue in service of others as well as in witness to God, because in and of themselves they model respect for those who are other and for those who are unknown. Celebrating the presence of Christ's body points us to the heart of who Anglicans are, wherever we are, and this continues to be true for us as Anglican Christians in inter-faith contexts. Because Christians themselves recognize that a presence which cannot be manifested openly cannot be encountered or engaged with, Christians seek to safeguard the principles of religious freedom for all. This is also recognized as central to human rights. The combined work of the Christ and the Spirit in all of this is powerfully expressed towards the end of *Generous Love* as follows: 'Nevertheless, as people who find healing through the broken body of Christ and confidence in the daring venture of the Spirit, we must not be deterred by the risk of failure or rejection.' This is the way in which presence and engagement combine both realism and generosity in inter-faith encounter.

Some reflective conclusions

From this flows a whole range of possibilities and honesties about inter-faith encounter:

- Being sent as emissaries of Christ Jesus in inter-faith encounter is the flip side of abiding as the body of Christ in places which are difficult. As Christ Jesus did this through his human birth, life, death and resurrection, his 'body language', we do it through the pattern of human personal response.
- Not all of this work is or can be done by those in the Church. In communicating the Spirit, we need to be willing to work with those other energetic forces of transformation in our societies. Practical projects and activities do, and will, draw us into working with those of quite different systems of belief. We are asked constantly to go the extra mile with and for those who reconcile people who are hurting and

who are causing hurt to others in contexts of rejection and exclusivity as well as radical incomprehension, contexts of confrontational secularism and also fundamentalism, however hard this word is to use.

- It is important not to rule inter-faith dialogue of ideas and dialogue of life out of mission. In fact this has not been the way of Christianity. *Generous Love* speaks carefully of the following cluster of ideas and activities: 'So evangelism belongs together with practical co-operation, work for reconciliation, and Inter-Faith dialogue, as all are ways of sharing in the energetic communication which is the mission of God's Spirit today.'

- Embassy and hospitality are closely intertwined as follows: 'The embassy which has been entrusted to us is the ministry of reconciliation, and the giving and receiving of hospitality is a most powerful sign that those who were strangers are reconciled to one another as friends.' *Generous Love* is very honest that 'true hospitality is not about concealing our convictions, but about expressing them in a practical way', and opens up the capacity of hospitality to transform meeting as such into sacred space. 'We come to learn that the spaces in which we meet one another do not ultimately belong to either host or guest; they belong to God, as do the so-called "neutral" spaces of public life.' Hence sacred and secular not only co-exist but interpenetrate one another; places of meeting are not the exclusive territory of any group; as part of creation they are God's given spaces where those made in God's image and likeness can meet.

- The challenge is to continue to seek and to find God in the difficult places. Our hope is that as we in good faith channel our energies into connection, communication and reconciliation with people of other faiths, we will open ourselves to the energy of the Holy Spirit of God and that they will reciprocate as both hosts and guests. *Generous Love*: 'Theology is always in tension with experience, and in Inter-Faith relations we need to live with provisionality, paradox and disappointment.'

A final thought

Inter-faith encounter will not go away. It is a part of life which encircles us and constantly challenges any excessively ecclesiastical understanding of life and of reality. We pray that the Church will live in the Spirit of the Christ and will seek to find the face of Christ in all the children of God. We hope that, in grasping some of the issues surrounding inter-faith encounter and dialogue, as Anglican Christians we can carry into parish and diocese some of the dynamism of the Lambeth Conference 2008 which was itself sustained and energized by generous love.

Bibliography

Hooker, Richard, c. 1592, *Laws of Ecclesiastical Polity Book 1*, in Ronald Bayne (ed.), *Laws of Ecclesiastical Polity Books 1–4*, London: J. M. Dent, 1907

10

ENGAGING WITH A MULTI-FAITH WORLD 3

Saw John Wilme

My country – Myanmar – is a very multi-faith context. At one of the world's most ancient crossroads of the major faith traditions, Buddhism, Christianity and Islam have long been in conversation here. Animism also maintains a major hold on people's outlook on life and the world. With 131 different ethnic groups sharing the space of our nation, each having its own traditional outlook and expression, an amazing combination of factors enters into our understanding of faith and action. But it was my sharing with fellow bishops in my Lambeth Conference *indaba* Group 1 that affirmed how extensively my church and I have already engaged the issues our multi-faith world presses upon us. This sharing also helped me understand and recognize the gifts and challenges of encountering each other on a daily basis as neighbours in community and as children of God cast in the divine likeness (Gen 1:27).

I was born and grew up in Thandaunggyi in south central Myanmar, not far now from the new national capital founded at Nay Pwi Taw. Thandaunggyi is a hill station where the Christian majority lives side by side with about 15 Hindu families and one Chinese Buddhist family. As children and teenagers, we enjoyed our lives together without any friction or difficulty even though we knew we held to different religions. Peacefully, and even happily, we enjoyed helping each other whenever our neighbours held their other religious activities and festivals, for neighbour-liness was a virtue dear to us, and our differences were of far lesser importance than kindness and community support. Perhaps our understanding and care for people of other faiths could be expressed simply according to Paul's appreciation written in his first letter to the Corinthians 13.11: 'When I was a child, I spoke like a child, I thought like a child, I reasoned like a child . . .' But later when I was a student of my Christian tradition at Holy Cross Theological College in Yangon (Rangoon) I began to think about these differences more seriously and began to won-der about my childhood and teenage years – did I do something wrong because I so enjoyed myself with friends of other faiths?

Later, after graduation and ordination, I served as a priest in Yangon from 1981 to 1994. One day a local government authority came to me to ask for a donation to support a Buddhist festival. I remember that while I did give a donation, I was uncomfort-able about it because I was more aware then that I was not only Christian but also a clergyman called to keep the Ten Command-ments (Exod. 20.4–17) and that 'you shall not bow down to any graven images'. Since we Christians had been taught that our Buddhist brothers and sisters were doing just that, I wondered, was I not supporting the worship of graven images?

Yet, when a Buddhist friend donated a carpet to our Holy Cross Theological College chapel, I wrote him a letter of thanks in which I quoted Luke 6.35: 'But love your enemies, do good and lend, ex-pecting nothing in return. Your reward will be great, and you will be children of the Most High, for he is kind to the unfaithful and the wicked.' A few days later the donor got in touch with me and continued to do so regularly until he converted to Christianity several months later. We Christians are happy to receive dona-tions from our friends of other faiths for support of our church programmes and activities and for the construction of our church buildings, but most of us will not give donations to their religious festivals, activities and programmes because we have been so edu-cated to fear breaking the first of the Ten Commandments.

After ministering in Yangon as Principal of Holy Cross Theo-logical College from 1989 until 1994, my young family and I moved north to Toungoo where I was consecrated to serve the people of God in Toungoo Diocese as their bishop, the servant of servants. There, much closer both to my childhood home and memories in Thandaunggyi, barely 30 miles away, I again recognized that my neighbours were Buddhist, Hindu, and Muslim as well as Christian, and that I had to encounter all of them on a daily basis as a good neighbour and newcomer to their community. How would I be salt and the light to my neighbours? How would I let my light so shine before them, that they might see my good works, and give glory to my Father in heaven (Matt. 5.13–16)? With the greater maturity of adulthood, I recognized that we Christians have to engage our multi-faith world by sharing our faith in service to all others in the context in which we find ourselves. In Toungoo, my family and I and my church constitute a distinct minority.

Being a minority religious community in Myanmar where the majority people are Buddhists officially supported by the government means that we Christians cannot easily talk with others about our religion or beliefs. Nor do we have any opportunity for official or even informal inter-faith dialogue. Dialogue of this kind is very difficult and even potentially dangerous for us because of the government's official support of Buddhism.

It is also very sensitive to talk about our faith because we are understood to be minorities who 'worship western religion'. Moreover, as Anglicans, we are identified with the British colonialists and remain officially connected with them through the Anglican Communion. Some of our churches still have signs that name them as 'the Church of England'! While we wish to work together with people of other faith communities and all people of good will, it is still almost impossible to do so with a complete sense of safety. Given circumstances like these, only when asked to do so do we dare speak for ourselves and share our faith.

However, I was indeed surprised to hear from foreigners that some believe we Christians of the Church in Myanmar are 'persecuted', because we truly are not. While we have suffered occasional discrimination and harassment because of our faith, we do officially enjoy freedom of worship. Even though we dare not declare in public settings that the God we believe in and worship is the one and only true God, the one in whom all human beings live, move, and have their being, as Paul declared when he addressed the pagan Athenians, we do find the freedom with which to declare the living God in our own contextual ways and means. For one, we seek to be visible and active within the wider community through the delivery of education, health and social care to all who come, and to do what we can in as faithful, charitable, and inoffensive ways as possible. When we are given an opening, we take every opportunity to share and proclaim our faith. We do so at community rites of passage at which our non-Christian neighbours are naturally present with us: funerals, weddings, and thanksgiving services become opportunities to show our traditions of worship and preach our beliefs and values without the usual fear of possibly being charged with attempts at conversion. As there are always friends of other faiths at these services of community interest and concern, we then take the opportunity boldly to proclaim the resurrection of our Lord Jesus Christ and to name Jesus as the Saviour of the world (e.g., 1 Cor. 15.12ff., John 11.25ff., John 3.16, etc.). So we manifest in our lives and ministries that Christianity is not a western religion, but also lives and moves and has its being naturally in our own native expressions, and we consider ourselves blessed to be able to share and express our faith by serving our broader inter-faith communities with our gifts and talents in ways like these.

One of the most successful examples of our service to the inter-faith community in which we live is our Agape Preschool. The Diocese started the Preschool in 1997. Now 85 per cent of the attending children of ages THREE to FIVE are from other faith families, and no matter their faith background, we encourage them to become good friends to all in the community. We have discovered that parents also regard us as their own good neighbours and friends. They willingly accept the given of Agape's Christian curriculum, which includes Christian prayers in the morning and evening, and the singing of Christian songs and memorization of Scripture verses. They apparently also look forward to and enjoy taking part in the school's annual Christmas party and in its

Thanksgiving and Graduation services. They even contribute to the expense of these special occasions at which we always share the message of our faith. By all counts, the school is a happy place and a success in multi-faith community. Parents accept it as an excellent place of training for their children's intellectual, physical, mental, and even spiritual development. They seem to feel and experience God's love and care through our lives and ministry, and they are able and willing to share with us in our expressions of Christian Spirit. It is heartening to have experienced that even or as teenagers the children often return upon special occasions as to reunions of old friends.

The Diocese is also running a small clinic which serves all who come, regardless of faith. We treated 3045 people from November 2007 to September 2008. Of the two doctors who work at the clinic, one is a Buddhist. A mobile diocesan medical team also visits our local villages every month to give treatment and health education to the community. Our teams give treatment and health education to between 100 and 150 people upon every village visit. People of other faiths say they have appreciated and recognized the teams' presence and service to them. We have seen that our friends of other faiths feel and experience God's love and healing through our clinical care and even invite their own friends and acquaintances to come for treatment with us because they trust us.

The Diocese is also running a Language Arts Centre. Every year, about 450 young people attend its various sessions. As with the preschool and clinic, the Centre serves all in the community regardless of faith and race, and more than 85 per cent of those who come are of other faiths. We know young people and their families appreciate our service and feel welcome and safe with us. Even though they regard Christianity as a western religion we see that the young people enjoy learning the English language, so we are trying our best to let them know and learn what Christianity is through this facility.

The Diocese is also running the Dorcas Sewing Training Centre to serve the community by developing sewing skills with which women can beautify their homes, lower their personal costs and even improve their family income. Since it was established, the Centre has trained hundreds of women of all faiths and ethnicities.

For over ten years Toungoo Diocese has also been providing materials and technical assistance to villages for safe water supply and sanitation, and has distributed mosquito nets for malaria prevention. We also assist in the area of education of young people by running boarding hostels and primary schools which are open to all regardless of faith and ethnicity. As with all our other programmes, we find that the people of our inter-faith community accept and support these ministries. They tell us they appreciate that the Church cares about them and is genuinely concerned about their needs. So we keep our great commandment and serve the Lord: 'Then the King shall say to those at his right hand, "Come, you that are blessed by my Father, inherit the kingdom prepared for you from the foundation of the world, for I was hungry and you gave me food, I was thirsty and you gave me something to drink, I was a stranger and you welcomed me, I was naked and you gave me clothing, I was sick and you took care of me, I was in prison and you visited me . . . Truly I tell you, just as you did it to the least of these who are members of my family, you did it to me"' (Matt 25:34–36; 40b).

The members of our *indaba* group also shared our thoughts about what the mission role of the bishop is and what role he/she plays specifically in inter-faith dialogue with people of other faiths and understandings. As noted, official and even unofficial dialogue is not only very difficult for us as minorities, it is almost practically impossible because of power struggles that occur when one side is supported politically and in turn, for its own political ends, supports the ruling group. For me, as a bishop one of the greatest of gifts and guides in my life and ministry is that since 1996, a local Muslim man who has a shop which sells household utensils has been a very close friend of mine and my family. I do not remember now how it was that I came to ask him to supervise the construction of the preschool that became our Agape Centre. Since then he has supervised the construction and repair of other diocesan church buildings, including our large new Diocesan Centre. We continue to do business together, not for ourselves but to benefit the Diocese. Having become good friends we often share our faith, sometimes very openly. We have talked a lot about our similarities, and of course there are many similarities between our faiths, a first step into true conversation. Gladly, we have even begun to talk about our religious differences, and with some wonder, because of the difficulty our context makes for both of us as minorities. We have even found that there is no problem at all in our sharing because of our friendship.

Our friendship was literally tested by fire when there was a conflict between Muslims and (some say) false Buddhist monks five years ago. When homes and shops were set on fire and the Muslim community feared for their lives, ten Muslim families came to us for refuge in our diocesan compound. It was a life and death situation for them and we welcomed them to safety inside our buildings. At that time I really admired my local neighbours – Buddhist, Hindu and Christian families – who also kept quiet and let the Muslims stay in our buildings without giving them away, even when people came to look over the walls to see if they were here. This was a great multi-faith community effort.

Our Muslim friends have never forgotten our love and care for them during that time. They now regard my family and the diocesan family who quietly cared for them and fed them as their good neighbours. They bring us gifts when they observe their religious festivals. My Muslim friend also brought his fiancée to our home before their marriage to seek my wife's and my counsel and advice. My wife and I still help them to have a happy married life. And we also visit them regularly. Faithful Christians and faithful Muslims – even though we do not believe in the same religion we are the children of God the Creator.

I also have a good Buddhist friend whom I have known for more than ten years. He was the mechanic who repaired our diocesan cars, and whenever we need help he gives us his assistance. One day he told me, 'Bishop, Christian children are very lucky. They have the opportunity to learn their religion every Sunday. But our Buddhist children do not have this opportunity.'

We have shared our faiths in friendship and regard each other as good friends. When we talk about our faith with our Muslim and Buddhist friends in the face of the kind of restrictions we all know and live with, we usually end by affirming that we are all made of the same flesh and blood, and for us all, compassionate love – the Myanmar speak of this love as *myittar* – is the most important value we share in our religious life.

Here in Myanmar there are many Christian groups who are very aggressive about evangelizing and converting people of other faiths. They are trying hard to keep and to fulfil the great commission (Mark 16.15–16). They are certainly trying hard to express and witness their faith in community worship and fellowship. But instead of coming to know Jesus as the saviour of the world, our neighbours of other faiths often experience their aggressive posture toward them and their attempts to convert them, and not understanding or accepting this approach, they often ask them to cease their worship and even entirely to close their churches and house churches. So nothing is gained, and much is lost.

Instances like this one make clear that there is a great need for education to help all baptized Christians understand how to engage with people of other faiths in ways that are sensitive, generous and neighbourly. Even though most of us usually feel uncomfortable talking about our faith, fearing that any conversation about religion might cause problems or even lead to the break-up of our friendships and relationships with others unlike ourselves, in order to share as we must in conversation, we first of all need to know our own beliefs better than we do. We also need to inform ourselves about the basic beliefs of others. How can we do this honestly?

In Myanmar, we Anglicans have intentionally shaped a new eucharistic liturgy that forms us to be a people called into newness of life in our inter-faith encounter and engagement with others in this multi-faith context in which we live as distinct minorities. We designed and introduced the 1999 *Order of Holy Communion* also to help people of other faiths better see us as children of God and not simply as ersatz westerners or native peoples who worship western religion. Using Trinitarian expres sions to state our faith in God the Father, God the Son and God the Holy Spirit, Creator, Redeemer and Sanctifier, we set our statements to parallel the threefold introductory statement Buddhists make about taking refuge in the Buddha, the Dhamma (Buddhist teaching) and the Sangha (the Monkhood) as they enter into their meditative discipline. So we also enter into worship with the opening acclamation, 'O God the Father, our Creator, we take refuge in you; O God the Son, our Redeemer, we take refuge in you; O God the Holy Spirit, we take refuge in you.' According to different seasons of the liturgical year, we also parallel basic Buddhist tenets of belief with our own almost creedal statements found in the Ten Commandments, the beginning of the Sermon on the Mount, and the Pauline statement found in 1 Corinthians 13.13 that 'faith, hope, and love abide, these three, but the greatest of these is love'. Coming as they do after the collect, these introduce the Ministry of the Word and secure for Christians that their minority belief is distinct yet not unsympathetic with the majority belief structures that surround them on every side. Effectively, then, these are all recognizably articulate, uncompromising Christian statements of faith that are also evangelistic in ways that are generous and neighbourly.

The Reverend Katharine E. Babson, a missionary of The Episcopal Church who serves her church and The Church of the Anglican Province of Myanmar as their official link as companions within the Anglican Communion, wrote about our new liturgy in *The Oxford Guide to The Book of Common Prayer: A Worldwide Survey*:

The Ten Commandments as the ethical foundation of the Christian's understanding of divine–human covenant, are used from Advent to Quinquagesima, the Sunday before Lent; from Lent to Whitsunday, the Day of Pentecost, 'The Eight Beatitudes'. This title ingeniously echoes the Buddhist principles of practical righteousness known as 'The Eightfold Path' – right *understanding*, right *thought*, right *speech*, right *action*, right *livelihood*, right *effort*, right *mindfulness*, and right *concentration*.

141

The Beatitudes do not match this list exactly, but Jesus' eight promises of blessedness are especially apt in light of the usual expectations of life in Myanmar today. They are statements of courage; they make plain the highest values and hopes Myanmar Christians have for all people in Myanmar; and, like the Ten Commandments, they are also proclamations of value to non-Christian Myanmar. In sum, they are evangelistic in every way. A third introduction to the Ministry of the Word is assigned throughout the Trinity season. Entitled 'The Three Virtues', it expands on the familiar triad of faith, hope and love, weaving it together with several other sentences drawn directly from scripture. As the 'Three Refuges' of Buddhism have even deeper, more complex levels of meaning, so too the 'Three Virtues', Paul's ultimate values, are here expounded and lead to a response that is yet another Biblical affirmation.

These three substantial innovations near the beginning of the Eucharistic liturgy are effectively confessions of faith that speak to the Buddhist cultural context in a Christian voice. (Babson: 2006, pp. 408–9)

Our minority religious life and experience in Myanmar tells us that the first, best, and most effective way to engage the multi-faith world is by sharing and expressing our faith through community service to others that honours their humanity, and incarnates Christ's presence among them. As ambassadors of Christ, we know our mission is to meet, greet, and acknowledge our dependence on our God whom we come to know better in Christ revealed in others. So it is that our community services are designed not to proclaim ourselves but to proclaim Jesus Christ as Lord and saviour of the world, and ourselves as his servants for the benefit of all. People of other faiths may be suspicious or fearful in the beginning of our friendship, but when we welcome them in all their difference we discover that we are truly enriched in the integrity of our faith by one another. We learn that there are spaces in which we can share and meet as friends and neighbours who were all created in God's image and so belong to God the Creator and Father of all. Knowing this, we listen carefully to our non-Christian neighbours even as we share our blessings with them. Giving, serving and receiving from each other is a most powerful sign for us of hope that a better community is still possible in our very constrained society. Indeed, in these ways, we learn that as we bear the fruits of the Spirit (Gal. 5.22) in our encounters with people of other faiths, we will be strengthened one day joyfully to engage the multi-faith world beyond our borders.

Finally, I believe inter-faith dialogue at the theological level is best exercised by scholars, but for those of us in the street and marketplace, the most important knowledge to guide us in our life with non-Christian others is to confess that all people are created in the image of God and are God's children. We Christians must acknowledge that we are called to discipleship in very different contexts. Daily we encounter increasing religious diversity and complexity in which we must do our best to engage the multi-faith world in order to promote God's kingdom, no matter whether we are numbered within the majority or the minority.

For us in Myanmar it may be that the unusual and forceful challenges and difficulties we face as minorities have taught us that we are called to witness Jesus Christ as Lord and proclaim our belief in the triune God in Christ-like service that is above all simple, wise, and gentle. We are to abide with our neighbours of different faiths as veritable signs of God's presence among them, and to engage our neighbours in all aspects of our daily lives as agents of God's mission to them and to the world, and to wonder how it is that God is working through them. In this troubled world that is ours in Myanmar, we know without doubt that God the Creator and Father of us all has been most generous in the opportunity, wisdom, and grace he has offered us in the cultural, ethnic, and religious diversity that is ours.

Bibliography

Babson, Katherine E., 'The Province of Myanmar (Burma)' in Charles Hefling and Cynthia Shattuck (eds.), *The Oxford Guide to The Book of Common Prayer: A Worldwide Survey*, Oxford: Oxford University Press, 2006

11

THE BISHOP AND LIVING UNDER SCRIPTURE

N. Thomas Wright

Introduction

My theme in this chapter has obviously been designed to go with the *indaba* group work on our use of the Bible.[1] This is an opportune time, as our Conference quickens its pace, to reflect on how we use Scripture, not least how we bishops use Scripture as part of our vocation, as in the main theme of this Conference, to be 'bishops in mission'.

Let me draw your attention to a book of mine which is foundational for what I'm going to say. *Scripture and the Authority of God* (Wright: 2005a) grew directly out of my work on both the Lambeth Commission and the International Anglican Theological and Doctrinal Commission. It was published in America under the strange title *The Last Word* (Wright: 2005b) – strange, because it certainly wasn't the last word on the subject, and also because if I were going to write a book called *The Last Word* I think it ought to be about Jesus Christ, not about the Bible. But such are the ways of publishers.

The puzzle about the book's title, though, points forward to the first thing I want to say, which is about the nature of biblical authority and the place of the Bible within the larger edifice of Christian theology and particularly missiology. I turn to my first main section.

Scripture and the authority of God

1. Scripture as the vehicle of God's authority

Debates about the authority of Scripture have tended to get off on the wrong foot and to turn into an unproductive shouting-match. This is partly because here, as in matters of political theology, in the words of Jim Wallis 'the Right gets it wrong and the Left doesn't get it' (Wallis: 2006). And sometimes the other way round as well. We have allowed our debates to be polarized within the false either/or of post-Enlightenment categories, so that we either see the Bible as a holy book, almost a magic book, in which we can simply look up detached answers to troubling questions, or see it within its historical context and therefore claim the right to relativize anything and everything we don't immediately like about it. These categories are themselves mistaken; the Bible itself helps us to challenge them; and when we probe deeper into the question 'What does it mean to say that the Bible is authoritative?' we discover a new and richer framework which simultaneously enables us to be deeply faithful to Scripture and energizes and shapes us, corporately and individually, for our urgent mission into tomorrow's world.

Consider: how does what we call 'the authority of the Bible' relate to the authority of God himself – and the authority of Jesus himself? When the risen Jesus commissions his followers for their worldwide mission, he does not say 'all authority in heaven and earth is given to – the books you people are going to go and write'. He says that all authority is given to him. When we say the closing words of the Lord's Prayer, we don't say that the kingdom, the power and the glory belong to the Bible, but to God himself. And when Jesus commissions the disciples for mission in John 20, he doesn't say 'receive this book' but 'receive the Holy Spirit'. Authority, then, has a Trinitarian shape and content. If we want to say, as I certainly want to say in line with our entire Anglican tradition, that the Bible is in some sense our authority, the Bible itself insists that that sentence must be read as a shorthand way of saying something a bit more complicated, something that will enable us to get some critical distance on the traditional shouting-match. From very early on in the Church, it became clear that those entrusted with God's mission included some who were called to write – to write letters on the one hand, and to collect, edit and write up the stories about Jesus, and the story of Jesus, on the other hand. The composition-criticism of the last few decades has moved us on a long way from the old half-truth that the biblical authors 'didn't think they were writing Scripture'. Paul certainly believed that God had entrusted him with an authoritative mission, and that his letter-writing formed part of that Spirit-given, Christ-shaped, kingdom-bringing activity. And the Gospel writers, in their different ways, write in such a manner as to say, with quite a rich artistry: here is the continuation and culmination of the great story you know from Israel's scriptures, and this is how, through its central character, it is now transformed into the narrative of God's dealings not just with Israel but with the whole world. Any first-century Jew who has the nerve to begin a book with 'In the beginning', weaving the themes of Genesis and Exodus, of Isaiah and the Psalms, into the story of Israel's Messiah, and doing so in such a way as to provide a framework around and energy for the mission and life of the followers of this Messiah – anyone who does something like this is either astonishingly un-self-aware or is making the definite claim to be writing something that corresponds, in a new mode, to the scriptural narrative of ancient Israel.

From very early on the first Christians discovered that the Church was to be shaped, and its mission and life taken forward, by the work of people who were called to write about Jesus, and about what it meant to follow him in his kingdom-mission. The new dispensation, the Messianic age, did not mean the abandonment of the notion of being shaped by a God-given book, but rather its transformation into something new, new genres and themes developing out of the old. But this already indicates that the Bible was not something detached, an entity apart from the Church, simply standing over against it. The Bible as we know it, Old and New Testaments, was, from the first, part of the life of God's people, and remained so as it was read in worship, studied in controversy, and made the basis for mission. But this did not mean then, and does not mean now, that the Bible can be twisted into whichever shape the Church wants at a particular time. You can't say, as some have tried to say, 'The Church wrote the Bible, so the Church can rewrite the Bible.' Paul would have had sharp words to say about that, as would the author of Revelation. From very early on, all the more powerful for being implicit and not yet much thought through, we find the first Christians living under Scripture, that is, believing that this book is its peculiar gift from its Lord, through the work of his Spirit, designed to enable the Church to be the Church, which is of course as we have been thinking throughout this Conference not a static thing but to be the Church in mission, to be sent into the world with the Good News of God's kingdom through the death and resurrection of his Son and in the power of that same Spirit.

2. God's authority and God's kingdom

When we say 'the authority of Scripture', then, we mean – if we know our business – God's authority, Christ's authority, somehow exercised through the Bible. But what is 'God's authority' all about? To look again at Scripture itself, it is clear that one of the most common models assumed by many in today's world simply won't do. We have lived for too long in the shadow of an older Deism in which God is imagined as a celestial CEO, sitting upstairs and handing down instructions from a great height. The Bible is then made to fit into the ontological and epistemological gap between God and ourselves; and, if it is the Deist God you are thinking of, that gap has a particular shape and implication. The Bible is then bound to become merely a source-book for true doctrines and right ethics. That is better than nothing, but it is always vulnerable to the charge, made frequently these days, that it is after all only an old book and that we've learnt a lot since then. The Left doesn't get it, and often all the Right can do is to respond with an ever more shrill repetition of 'the

Bible, the Bible, the Bible'. As the late great Phil Ochs sang during Vietnam,

> And they argue through the night,
> Black is black and white is white,
> And walk away both knowing they are right;
> And nobody's buying flowers from the flower lady.

I know that quoting a Vietnam protest song dates me, but I guess
that I'm not the only one in this room radically shaped by the
events of the late 1960s . . .

The real problem with the Deism that infected so much of the
western world in the eighteenth century and dominates it still
– thank God for our brothers and sisters from elsewhere who
didn't have that problem! – is that it lives by serious reaction
against the whole notion of God's kingdom coming 'on earth
as in heaven'. (Actually, much Protestant theology couldn't really cope with this idea either, perhaps in reaction against the
perceived worldly kingdom of medieval Catholicism, which is
why it privileged a particular reading of St Paul over against
the Gospels, a problem still with us in the guise of the Bultman-
nian legacy.) But when we re-read the Gospels and the kingdom-
announcement we find there into the centre of our own life and
thought, we discover that God is not a distant faceless bureau-
crat handing down 'to do' lists, our 'commands for the day'. The
God of Scripture is with us in the world, his world, the world in
which he lived and died and rose again in the person of his Son,
in which he breathes new life through the person of his Spirit.
Scripture is the vehicle of the kingdom-bringing 'authority', in
that sense, of this God. That is why the Left, which prefers a detached Deism so it can get on and do its own thing, disregarding
instructions that seem to come from a distant God or a distant
past, gets it wrong, and why the Right, which wants an authoritarian command from on high, doesn't get it.

There is a particular problem here, because our Anglican formularies speak of Scripture and its authority in terms of 'things
which are to be believed for eternal salvation'. Living as they did

within the late medieval western view, our Anglican fathers rightly saw Scripture as the norm which guided you towards God's promised salvation through faith in Jesus Christ; but, like everyone else at the time, they saw that salvation less in terms of God's kingdom coming on earth as in heaven and more in terms of being rescued from this earth for a 'salvation' somewhere else. We can't go into this in any detail, but I just want to note that part of the exciting work today of re-integrating Gospels and epistles and rethinking the whole notion of the kingdom and particularly new creation and resurrection is not without its effect on the place and role of Scripture in the whole process. Basically, I believe that Scripture is the book through which the Church is enabled to be the Church, to be the people of God anticipating his sovereign rule on earth as in heaven, and that this fleshes out what our formularies say in a three-dimensional and energetic fashion.

3. Scripture and the story of God's mission

So how does the Bible function in the way I have described? Answer: by being itself; and 'being itself' means, primarily, being itself as story. I do not mean by this what some have seen as 'mere story', that is, a cheerfully fictive account to be relegated to the world of 'myth'. The Christian Bible we know is a quite astonishingly complete story, from Chaos to Order, from first creation to new creation, from the Garden to the City, from covenant to renewed covenant, and all fitting together in a way that none of the authors can have seen but which we, standing back from the finished product, can only marvel at. Speaking as a student of ancient literature, I am continually astonished by the shape of Scripture, which can't simply be explained away as the product of some clever decisions by a third- or fourth-century Council. Of course Scripture contains many sub-plots, and many parts which are not in themselves 'narrative' at all – poems, meditations, wisdom sayings, and so on. But the narrative shape continues to stand out, and indeed to stand over against all attempts to flatten Scripture out either into a puzzle-book of secret gnostic wisdom, which deconstructs the stories, or into a book of true

answers to dogmatic and ethical questions, which also deconstructs the stories but from a different angle.

And this raises the question, how can a narrative be authoritative? This is the right question to ask, and it raises some exciting
possibilities. As I have set out at length elsewhere, Scripture offers precisely the unfinished narrative of God's heaven-and-earth
project, God's great design, as Paul puts it, echoing the Law and
the Prophets, to join everything in heaven and earth into one in
Christ. And the unfinished narrative functions like an unfinished
play, in which those who belong to Jesus Christ are now called
to be the actors, taking forward the drama towards its intended
conclusion. This is actually a far stronger, and more robust, ver-
sion of 'authority' than the one which simply imagines the Bible
as a source-book for true dogmatic and ethical propositions. Of
course such propositions are to be found in it, and they matter; but they matter as the tips of a much, much larger iceberg,
which is the entire drama. And it is by soaking ourselves in that
whole drama that we, God's people in Christ Jesus, are to live
with and under Scripture's authority, not simply by knowing
which bits to look up on which topics, but by becoming people
of this story, people formed and shaped in our imaginations and
intuitions by the overall narrative, so that we come to know by
second nature not only what Scripture says on particular topics
but why it says those things. And living under scriptural authority, contrary to what has been said by liberalism ever since the
eighteenth century, does not then mean being kept in an infantile
state, shut up parroting an ancient text, but rather coming alive,
growing up, taking responsibility for seeing how the narrative
has gone forward and where it must go next. We are, in short,
to be improvisers, which as any musician knows doesn't mean
playing out of tune or out of time but rather discerning what is
appropriate in terms of the story so far and the story's intended
conclusion.

This, I submit, has a strong claim to be an intrinsically Anglican way of thinking about Scripture, insofar as there can be said
to be such a thing. I am always intrinsically suspicious of claims
to discover a specifically or intrinsically Anglican approach to

anything, not just because of the myriad of local variations but because of the characteristic Anglican claim that Anglicans have no specific doctrine of their own – it's just that if something is true, Anglicans believe it. The truth behind that old joke is that we have tried over the years, when it comes to Scripture at least, to nourish a tradition of careful scholarship, rooted in philology, history and the early Fathers, hand in hand with a readiness to let the Bible resonate in new ways in new situations. As an example of this I cherish Brooke Foss Westcott, Bishop of Durham a hundred and ten years ago, who is buried close to J. B. Lightfoot in the great chapel at Auckland Castle. Westcott is known, of course, for his meticulous textual criticism, and his magisterial commentaries on John and Hebrews. But in Durham he is also remembered for being the bishop who, before the days of trade unions, settled a long and damaging miners' strike by negotiating so hard with the mine owners that eventually they met the workers' demands. For Westcott, careful biblical scholarship and hard street-level work for God's kingdom were two parts of the same whole, and we should be proud when Anglicanism reflects similar combinations.

All this is of course nurtured by the straightforward but deeply powerful tradition of the daily offices, with the great narratives of Scripture read through day by day, preferably on a *lectio continua* basis, so that 'living prayerfully within the story' is the most formative thing, next to the Eucharist itself, which Anglicans do. Classic mattins and evensong, in fact, are basically showcases for Scripture, and the point of reading Old and New Testaments like that is not so much to 'remind ourselves of that bit of the Bible', as to use that small selection as a window through which we can see, with the eyes of mind and heart, the entire sweep of the whole Bible, so that our 'telling of the story' is not actually aimed primarily at informing or reminding one another but rather at praising God for his mighty acts, and acquiring the habit of living within the story of them as we do so. That, I suggest, is the heart of Anglican Bible study.

Seeing the Bible in terms of its great story enables us, in particular, to develop a layered and nuanced hermeneutic which retains the full authority of the whole Bible while enabling us to understand why it is, for instance, that some parts of the Old Testament are still directly relevant to us while others are not, and how this is not arbitrary but rooted in serious theological and exegetical principle. In the book I have developed the model of the five-act play, with Creation and Fall as the first two acts, then Israel, then Jesus himself, and then the act in which we ourselves are still living, whose final scene we know from passages like Romans 8, 1 Corinthians 15 and Revelation 21 and 22. The point of this model is partly to explain the notion of 'improvising' I mentioned earlier – when living within the fifth act, we are required to improvise our way to the necessary conclusion while remaining completely faithful to the narrative, and the characterizations, of the earlier acts and indeed to the opening scenes of our own present act, i.e. Easter and Pentecost. But it is also partly to provide a way of understanding how it is that though, for instance, the book of Leviticus is part of our story, a non-negotiable part of that story, it is not the part where we presently live. When you live in Act 5, you cannot repeat, except for very special effect, a speech which was made in Act 3. Thus we do not offer animal sacrifice; the letter to the Hebrews makes that abundantly clear. A similar argument is mounted by Paul in Galatians about God's gift of the Mosaic law: it was good and God-given, but those of its prescriptions which separate out Jews from Gentiles are no longer appropriate, since we are not any longer in Act 3 but in Act 5, and with that eschatological moment the old distinctions are done away. This could be pursued at much greater length, but let me just make one particular and important point. There are of course a good many features of the Pentateuch which are not only retained but enhanced in the New Testament; one cannot assume because some features of Mosaic law are abolished that all are equally redundant, just as it would be a bad mistake to suppose that the reason some parts have become redundant is simply because they're old or because we now 'know better'. Things are not that shallow. In fact, it gradually becomes clear that the OT is continually calling Israel to a way of life which is about discovering a genuinely human existence, and that, granted the achievement of Jesus the Messiah in Act 4, a good many features of the Mosaic law are not only retained but enhanced. This holds true for the Decalogue itself, with the sole exception of the sabbath law, and it certainly holds for the codes of sexual conduct, as a great wealth of scholarship has shown again and again. In the whole Bible, what men and women do sexually resonates with larger cosmic issues, and particular commands and prohibitions are not arbitrary, detached rules, but tip-of-the-iceberg features revealing a deep and structured worldview underneath. I commend the five-act model to you as a creative and fresh way of understanding and using the Bible for all it's worth.

But it is of course particularly designed to explain how the great story of the Bible is designed to point us to our mission and to equip us precisely for that mission. The story begins with the creation of heaven and earth, and it ends with their eventual marriage, their coming together in fulfilling, God-ordained union. The biblical story reaches its climax of course in Jesus Christ, where this union of heaven and earth was inaugurated, modelled and accomplished – against all the powers that would keep them apart – through his death and resurrection. And the mission of the Church in the power of the Spirit is to implement the achievement of Jesus and so to anticipate the eventual goal. Mission, in other words, takes place within the overall narrative of Scripture, and is reinforced and kept in place by the reading and studying of the text that speaks this way, drawing together all features of wider culture that point in this direction and standing over against all features of wider culture which point elsewhere. It is only by living within this overall narrative that we, as bishops committed to leading the Church in mission, can keep our bearings when so many elements of our own culture and our various traditions would threaten to sidetrack us this way or that. As I have written elsewhere, the larger biblical narrative offers us a framework for developing and taking forward a holistic mission which refuses to split apart full-on evangelism, telling people about Jesus with a view to bringing them to faith, and full-on kingdom-of-God work, labouring alongside anyone and everyone with a heart for the Common Good so that God's sovereign and saving rule may be glimpsed on earth as in heaven.

Anglicanism has tended to oscillate between these two, between a primary reading of the epistles as being about private and personal salvation and a primary reading of the Gospels as being about 'social justice'. The two need one another, and in the best Anglican traditions they join up, like all the other complementarities in God's world. So my point at this stage is this: a serious Anglican reading of Scripture can and should generate a five-act hermeneutic in which our goals in mission are greatly clarified and our energy and sense of direction for that mission reinforced, as the Spirit uses our telling and retelling of the story to shape the habits of our hearts, minds and wills. And to say that is of course to say that, at the very heart of it all, the point of Scripture is to root, form and shape our spirituality as a people and as individuals. We are to be a Scripture-shaped praying people, which of course means a Jesus-shaped praying people, which of course includes being a Scripture-shaped and Jesus-shaped eucharistic people. It is out of that scripturally formed well of personal and corporate spirituality, continually confronting, transforming and directing us, that we draw water to be refreshed as we find our way forward in the service of God, his gospel and his kingdom. But all this points us on to our present culture and the challenges it presents. How can Scripture form us for mission in tomorrow's world?

Scripture and the task of the Church

1. *Foundation: Bible and culture*

The confrontation between Christian faith and contemporary culture, between (if you like) Jerusalem and Athens, is as old as the gospel itself. It is rooted in turn in the confrontation between the Old Testament people of God and the surrounding cultures of Egypt, Canaan, Assyria, Babylon and then, later, Persia, Greece, Syria and eventually Rome. Indeed, cultural confrontation and the complex negotiations it generated are woven into the very fabric of Scripture itself. Jonathan Sacks, who we so revelled in listening to last night, wrote an article the other day[2] about the way in which languages without vowels, such as Hebrew, tend to go from right to left, driven by right-brain intuition, whereas languages with vowels, such as Greek, tend to go from left to right, as the left-brain passion for getting things worked out accurately drives from that side. I asked him at dinner whether he'd had any feedback on the article, and he said rather disappointedly that he hadn't; but he drew the moral, which I now develop, that part of the power of the early Christian faith was to take a right-brain religion such as Judaism and express it within a left-brain language like Greek. (Of course, you could argue that the Rabbis made up for lost left-brain time with the Mishnah and Talmud, but that would be another story.) From the very beginning, Christianity was engaged with its many surrounding cultures, and no one model – Niebuhr, you recall, explored five in his classic book *Christ and Culture* (Niebuhr: 1952) – will catch all the nuances we might wish.

Even in a short address such as Paul's on the Areopagus (Acts 17.22–31) we can see all kinds of different things going on. Paul is in head-on collision with the great temples all around him, and the endless stream of sacrifices being offered at them, yet he can begin from the Altar to the Unknown God and work up from there, quoting Greek poets on the way. And, reading between the lines, we can see how the message he brought could say both Yes and No to the Stoic, the Epicurean and the Academic. The Stoic supposes that all is predetermined, that divinity is simply suffused within the world and working its purpose out. Well, says Paul, you are right that God is not far from any of us, but wrong to suppose that God and the world are the same thing. The Epicurean supposes that God, or the gods, are a long way away, and that the best thing to do is make such shift as we can in this world. Well, says Paul, you are right that God and the world are not the same thing, but you are wrong to suppose that God is not interested in the world, and us human creatures. The Academic sits on the fence: there isn't really enough evidence to be sure about the gods, so it's best to keep the old state religion going just in case (a position not unfamiliar, alas, to some Anglicans). Well, says Paul, you are right that there hasn't really been quite enough evidence to be sure of anything; but now all that has changed, because there is a man called Jesus whom God raised from the dead, and he is going to sort everything out from top to bottom.

Now of course the point of all that is not simply an interesting set of skirmishes about different ideas. The point is that these ideas had legs, and went about in the ancient world making things happen. They altered the way you saw things, the way you did things, the goals you set yourself and the ways you ordered your world and society. From the beginning no serious Christian has been able to say 'this is my culture, so I must adapt the gospel to fit within it', just as no serious Christian has been able to say 'this is my surrounding culture, so I must oppose it tooth and nail'. Christians are neither chameleons, changing colour to suit their surroundings, nor rhinoceroses, ready to charge at anything in sight. There is no straightforward transference between any item of ordinary culture and the gospel, since all has been distorted by evil; but likewise there is nothing so twisted that it cannot be redeemed, and nothing evil in itself. The Christian is thus committed, precisely as a careful reader of Scripture, to a nuanced reading of culture and a nuanced understanding of the response of the gospel to different elements of culture. You can see this in Philippians, where Paul is clear that as a Christian you must live your public life in a manner worthy of the gospel, and that whatever is pure, lovely and of good report must be celebrated – but also that Jesus is Lord while Caesar isn't, and that we are commanded to shine like lights in a dark world. There are no short cuts here, no easy answers. Prayer, Scripture and complex negotiation are the order of the day.

There is of course a very particular Anglican spin to some of this. Many parts of the older Anglican world, not least here in England itself, have become very used to going with the flow of the culture, on the older assumption that basically England was a Christian country so that the Church would not be compromised if it reflected the local social and cultural mores. That strand of Anglicanism has always been in danger of simply acting as chaplain to whatever happened to be going on at the time, whether it was blessing bombs and bullets in the First World War or going to tea at Buckingham Palace. Within that world, the Bible has often been quietly truncated. We don't like the bits about judgement, so we miss them out. We are embarrassed by the bits about sex, so we miss them out too – and then we wonder why, in a world full of hell and sex, people imagine the Bible is irrelevant! The Bible is a kind of spiritual Rorschach test: if you find you're cutting bits out, or adding bits in, it may be a sign that you're capitulating to cultural pressure. Equally, of course, there are many parts of the Anglican world where nothing but confrontation has been possible for a long time, and there people may have to learn the difficult lesson that actually the world is still charged with the grandeur of God, and that the biblical Christian must learn to rejoice with those who rejoice and weep with those who weep, no matter who they are, what they believe or how they behave. It is crucial to our vocation, and to our particular vocation granted our particular histories, that we rediscover the art, which itself is rooted in Scripture, of discriminating (as Paul says) between things that differ, and of affirming what can and must be affirmed and opposing what can and must be opposed. Those of us who are involved in the business of politics and government know that this is a difficult and often thankless task, but it must be undertaken.

2. *The Bible and Gnosticism*

All this brings us to three particular features of tomorrow's world which stand out particularly and call for a biblical engagement as we take forward our God-given mission. I am here summarizing the Noble Lectures I was privileged to give at Harvard University two years ago, which are yet to be published. The three features are Gnosticism, Empire and postmodernity, which fit together in fascinating ways and which provide a grid of cultural and personal worldviews within which a great many of our contemporaries live today. I speak particularly of the western world, and I regret that I am not qualified to do more of a 'world tour'. But I remind all of us that, whether we like it or not, when the West sneezes everyone else catches a cold, so that cultural trends in Europe and North America will affect the whole world. (I notice that, though the current American election will affect everybody on the face of the earth for good or ill, only Americans get to vote. This strikes me as odd, though of course we British were in the same position for long enough and didn't seem to mind at the time.)

Addressing these three issues could sound like an abstract intellectual exercise, but believe me it isn't. This is the real world where people struggle and sin and suffer, and it is fatally easy for the Church to be pulled down into the cultural assumptions of the day and so have no gospel, nothing to offer, no basis for mission or content to it either.

The first of the three makes this point graphically. When I was in college we studied Gnosticism as a strange ancient phenomenon, little imagining that it was already alive and well in western culture and that it would sweep through our world dramatically, not only in obvious things like *The Da Vinci Code* but in the subtext of half the Hollywood movies and, more sadly, half the would-be theological thinking in our church. Two features stand out. First a radical dualism, in which the created order is irrelevant because we, the enlightened ones, are just passing through it and can use or ignore it as we please. At this point the Gnosticism of the right says, we can do what we like with our planet, because it's all going to be destroyed soon and we'll be snatched away to a distant heaven. And the Gnosticism of the left says, we can do what we like with our bodies, because they are irrelevant to the reality within us. And both are held in place by the larger Gnosticism of the western Enlightenment itself which has said, for the last two hundred years, we westerners are the enlightened ones, with our modern science and technology; we can make up the rules, we can saunter around the world exploiting its resources and its people, we can drop bombs on people to make whole countries do what we want, and it doesn't matter much because we, the enlightened ones, are the natural possessors of justice, freedom and peace so those other people don't matter as much as we do.

Along with the radical dualism goes Gnosticism as a religion, not of redemption, but of self-discovery. This is the real 'false gospel' at the heart of a good many contemporary debates. The Gnostic does not want to be rescued; he or she wants to discover 'who they really are', the inner spark of divine life. There is even a danger that we Anglicans spend time discussing 'who we really are', as though there were some inner thing, the Anglican spark, and if only we could identify that then we'd be all right. And in some of our most crucial ethical debates people have assumed for a long time that 'being true to myself' was all that really mattered (at this point the existentialism and romanticism of the last two hundred years reinforce the underlying Gnosticism). This is a religion of pride rather than of faith, of self-assertion rather than of hope, of a self-love which is a parody of the genuinely biblical self-love which is regard for oneself, body and all, as reflecting the image of the creator.

And this false religion, though it often uses the language of Christianity, makes it impossible for people to have real Christian faith, or for that matter real Jewish faith; because in the Bible you discover 'who you really are' only when the living God, the creator, is rescuing you and giving you a new identity, a new status, a new name. The Bible is itself the story of, and the energy to bring about, the redemption of creation, ourselves included, not the discovery within ourselves of a spark which just needs to express itself. Gnosticism hates resurrection, because resurrection speaks of God doing a new thing within and for the material world, putting it right at last, rather than God throwing the material world away and allowing the divine spark to float off free. And it is resurrection – the resurrection of Jesus in the past, and of ourselves in the future – which is the ground of all Christian ethical life in the present. Christian ethics is not a matter of 'discovering who you truly are' and then being true to that. It is a matter, as Jesus and Paul insist, of dying to self and coming alive to God, of taking up the cross, of inaugurated eschatology, of becoming in oneself not 'what one really is' already but 'what one is in Christ', a new creation, a small, walking, breathing anticipation of the promised time when the earth shall be filled with God's glory as the waters cover the sea. A biblically based mission must learn from the great narrative of Scripture to set its face against all Gnosticism, because it cuts the nerve of the mission both to the world of politics and society and to the life of every man, woman and child.

3. The Bible and Empire

Second, Empire. We British had an empire on which the sun never set, and we have spent the last hundred years puzzling over what went wrong and counting the cost. As I have said often enough, I hope and pray my beloved American friends don't have to do the same. Let's be clear: there is nothing absolutely wrong with empire in itself; empires come and go, they always have done, and the point is not 'Wouldn't it be a better world without empires at all?' but 'How can empires be called to account, be reminded that God is God and that they are not?' All empires declare that they possess justice, freedom and peace; Greece did it, Rome did it, the British did it a century ago, the Americans do it now. Who will be next, and are we ready for that with a biblical narrative of empire that will say, with Colossians 1, that all the powers in heaven and on earth were created in and through and for Jesus Christ and were redeemed by the blood of his cross? Are we ready, in our biblically shaped mission, to transcend the futile rhetoric of left and right – a very recent invention, in fact itself an invention of the Enlightenment – and to understand power the way the Bible understands it, as given by God to bring order to his creation on the one hand and, on the other, to anticipate in the present that final putting-to-rights of all things which we are promised?

If we are thinking biblically we have a narrative which encodes a mission, the mission of God both to the rulers of this age and to those whose lives are either enhanced by them or crushed by them, or quite often simply confused by them in the middle. We in the West need to learn from our brothers and sisters who live under regimes which are deeply hostile to the Church and would prefer that it disappeared altogether. And, dare I say, we need to learn these lessons quite quickly, because people are already talking about the next great superpower, and whether it is India or China we can be sure that, unless something truly extraordinary happens, the world will be dominated for the first time since ancient Rome by a superpower that does not stand within the Judaeo-Christian tradition, and which will see that tradition as a threat. If we don't prepare ourselves now for the future reality, and if we don't learn the biblical lessons here and now of what Christian mission looks like under empire, we will fail not only the world of our own day but also the world of our children's and grandchildren's day.

Notice how empire and Gnosticism go together. Gnosticism arises under empire, because when you are powerless to change anything about your world you are tempted to turn inwards and suppose that a spiritual, inner reality is all that matters. Carl Jung put it nicely if chillingly: who looks outside, dreams; who looks inside, awakens. Welcome to the world of navel-gazing. That's why second-century Gnosticism arose when it did, following the collapse of the final Jewish revolt in AD 135. And the empires of the world are delighted when people embrace Gnosticism. Again in the second century the people who were reading the Gospel of Thomas and other books of the same sort were not burnt at the stake or thrown to the lions. That was reserved for the people who were reading Matthew, Mark, Luke, John and the rest. There is a massive lie out there at the moment, which is that the canon of Scripture colludes with imperial power while the Gnostic literature subverts it. That is the exact opposite of the truth. Caesar couldn't care less if someone wants to pursue a private spirituality. But if they go around saying that all authority in heaven and on earth is given to the crucified and risen Jesus, Caesar shivers in his shoes. And going around saying that is at the heart of Christian mission, which is sustained and energized by Scripture itself, the book that will keep not only individual Christians but whole churches steadfast and cheerful in that mission when everything seems bent on blowing them off course.

4. *Postmodernity*

Whenever I mention postmodernity my wife either groans or yawns, but before you have those same reactions let me say what I mean. We live in a world – the western world, but increasingly the global community – where truth is at a discount. Relativism is everywhere; there is only 'your truth' and 'my truth'. Facts don't matter, spin is all that counts. Likewise, and deeply worrying for the Church, because we easily get sucked into this, argument and reason are set aside, and instead of debate we have the shrill swapping of hurt emotions. 'I am a victim; you are prejudiced; end of conversation.' Or, in one of those worrying irregular verbs, 'I am speaking from the heart, you are prejudiced, he or she is a bigot.' My friends, this entire way of thinking – a world where the only apparent moral argument is the volume of the victim's scream – is an affront to the biblical world, to the Anglican world, to the world of Scripture, tradition and reason. Reason is not the same as emotion or indeed experience. Genuine screams of genuine victims matter enormously, of course, and are all taken up into the cry of dereliction from the cross. But they are to be addressed, not with more screams, still less competing ones, but with healing, biblical wisdom. The reaction against Scripture within postmodern Christianity is no worse than the reaction against reason itself. And 'experience', which for John Wesley when he elevated it alongside Scripture, tradition and reason meant 'the experience of God the Spirit at work transforming my life', has come to mean 'whatever I feel' – which is no more a safe guide to anything than a glance at the English sky in the morning is a safe guide to the weather later in the day.

Of course, postmodernity doesn't stop with the deconstruction of truth. It deconstructs the self as well. At this point the Gnostic would do well to hide, because in postmodernity there is no such thing as the inner spark, the true inward reality. That's why, for instance, in today's debates among the gay community, the essentialist position ('this is who I am') is increasingly discounted by the constructivists ('this is what I choose to be today') – though you wouldn't know that from the way the Church still talks about the matter. But the greatest deconstruction of all is of course that of the overarching narrative, the great stories. Big stories, like truth-claims, declares the postmodernist, are claims to power. Live within the modernist story and the modernists will end up running the show. That's how the world has worked for long enough.

And of course that presents quite a challenge to the Christian; because the Bible, as I have stressed, is precisely a great narrative, the huge, sprawling story of creation and new creation, of covenant and new covenant, with Jesus in the middle of it. That is why many Christians today shrink their mission to the mere attempt to give some people, here and there, a spiritual life and a hope out beyond, rather than taking the mission where it needs to go, into every corner of God's world and its systems and structures. But please note: the deconstruction of power-stories is itself a claim to power. Pontius Pilate asked Jesus 'What is truth?' because for him the only truth was what came out of the scabbard of a sword. Indeed, the conversation between Jesus and Pilate in John 18 and 19 stands near the heart of a biblical theology of mission, though sadly I'm not sure if that will come out in our Bible Studies in the next few days. In other words, though postmodernism sneers at empire and its grandiose dreams, in the final analysis it colludes with it. It can scoff, but it cannot subvert. All those years of Jacques Derrida, and we still got George Bush. And Tony Blair.

So what does the Bible itself have to say on the matter? How can the great story I've been speaking of respond to the postmodern challenge – because make no mistake, if it doesn't, our mission will shrink into a sad little parody of its true self. The answer is that the story of Scripture is not a story of power, but a story of love – genuine love, overflowing love for the world God made. Note carefully what happens at this point.

I said postmodernity had one moral value only, the scream of the victim. That isn't quite true. It has one other: the duty to, as is often said, 'embrace the Other'. This has come from various sources and it's sometimes joined up, though I have to say with minimal justification, with some elements of the work of Jesus. This is at the heart of the appeal that we 'live with difference', and so on. I have spoken about that elsewhere; it all depends on a decision as to which differences you can and should live with and which you shouldn't and can't. There is an enormous amount of begging the question currently on this matter. But when we consider the biblical narrative we discover that here again postmodernity has produced a parody of the reality. In Scripture, God makes a world that is other than himself, and that is full of complementarities: heaven and earth, night and day, sea and land, vegetation and animals, and ultimately humans, with the complementarity of male and female growing more evident within that world until it is finally affirmed, producing a picture of a world of radical differences with the differences made for one another. Within the biblical narrative, of course, this reaches its great conclusion when heaven and earth finally come together, with the new Jerusalem as the bride of Christ. This is the biblical story of love: the love of God for his world, the love within that world for that which is radically different from me, from us, the love which really does 'embrace the other', not in a casual and floppy sense of 'anyone who's a bit different from me', but in the deep ontological sense of a love which goes out into a different country altogether to affirm the goodness of God's creation there and to discover, in that affirmation, the greatest delight which mirrors the delight of God the creator, the delight of Christ the lover.

What we desperately need, if we are to pursue a biblical, Christian and indeed Anglican mission in the postmodern world, is the Spirit of Truth. There is no time to develop this further, but it is vital to say this one thing. We have got so used to the postmodern sneer that any truth-claim is instantly suspect. And at that point many Christians have lurched back to the apparent safety of a modernist claim: conservative modernists claim that they can simply look up truth in the Bible, without realizing what sort of book it is, while radical modernists claim they find truth in today's science, without realizing what sort of a thing that is either. But we cannot go back; we have to go on; and the Spirit of Truth, often invoked in favour of any and every innovation in the Church, is actually at work when we live within the great story, the love story, God's love story, and become in turn agents, missional agents, of that story in the world. Truth is not something we possess and put in our pockets, because truth is grounded in the goodness of creation, the promise of redemption for that creation, and the vocation of human beings to speak God's word both of naming the original creation and of working for new creation – the word, in other words, of mission. The Spirit of Truth is given so that, living within the great biblical story, we can engage in those tasks.

Conclusion

There is much more to say, as Jesus himself said in the Farewell Discourses, but you cannot bear it now. I hope I have said enough to spark off some discussion and open up some topics of more than a little relevance to who we are as bishops in the Anglican Communion and what we should be about in our mission in tomorrow's world. I have tried to offer a robust account of the way in which the Bible is designed to be the vehicle of God's authority, not in an abstract sense but in the dynamic sense of the story through which God's mission in the world goes forward in the power of the Spirit. And within that larger picture, the small details slot into place, not as isolated fragments of disjointed moral or theological musings, but, as I said before, as tips of the iceberg which show what is there all along just under the surface. There are other questions I haven't addressed, not least the way in which the Bible demands to be read both individually and corporately in each generation, so that each generation can grow up intellectually, morally, culturally and Christianly. We will never get to the point where scholarship has said all that needs to be said and subsequent generations will just have to look up the right answers. Thank God it isn't like that. But, as we in turn give ourselves to the tasks of being bishops-in-mission, of being biblical-bishops-in-mission, we must always remind ourselves that the Bible is most truly itself when it is being, through the work of God's praying people and not least their wise shepherds, the vehicle of God's saving, new-creational love going out, not to tell the world it is more or less all right as it is, but to do for the whole creation, and every man, woman and child within it, what God did for the children of Israel in Egypt, and what God did for the world in the death and resurrection of Jesus: to say 'I have heard your crying, and I have come to the rescue.'

Bibliography

Niebuhr, Richard H., *Christ and Culture*, London: Faber and Faber, 1952

Wallis, Jim, *God's Politics: Why the Right Gets it Wrong and the Left Doesn't Get it*, San Francisco: HarperCollins, 2006

Wright, N. T., *Scripture and the Authority of God*, London: SPCK, 2005a

Wright, N. T., *The Last Word: Scripture and the Authority of God*, San Francisco: HarperCollins, 2005b

Notes

1 This text was originally prepared for the *indaba* group on the use of the Bible at the Lambeth Conference 2008.

2 'Credo: The Right Hemisphere of the Brain Knits it all Tgthr', 4 July 2008, *The Times*, available at http://www.timesonline.co.uk/tol/comment/faith/article4272143.ece

12

EQUIPPING FOR GOD'S MISSION

The Missiological Vision of the 2008 Lambeth Conference of Anglican Bishops[1]

Ian T. Douglas

The decennial meeting of bishops of the worldwide Anglican Communion known as the Lambeth Conference has never been immune from controversy. Archbishop of Canterbury Charles Longley called for the first Lambeth Conference in 1867, in part, to consider if John Colenso, Bishop of Natal in South Africa, had gone too far in his accommodations of Scripture and the teachings of the Church to Zulu culture (Ward: 2006, pp. 139–41). While the 'Colenso Affair' itself had significant missiological implications, namely how far would Anglican understandings of Scripture and the authority of the local church embrace change in response to new contexts, the nature of the Conference itself was also controversial. Not wanting to give credence to a centralization of Episcopal power in what some might perceive as a new kind of council or synod of bishops within Anglicanism, the then Archbishop of York and the Bishop of Durham, two of the most senior bishops in the Church of England, refused to attend (Chadwick: 1992, pp. v–vii). Thus questions related to scriptural interpretation, the nature of the Church, the authority of the Lambeth Conference itself, and the lack of participation by some key bishops, all of which swirled around the fourteenth Lambeth Conference held in Canterbury, England from 16 July to 3 August 2008 were not at all new to this global gathering of Anglican bishops.

What was new for the 2008 Lambeth Conference was how the Conference chose to address these difficult issues. Eschewing established processes the 2008 Lambeth Conference pursued a decidedly missiological vision in its design, processes, and content. The Design Group for the Conference was motivated by a belief that the mission of God is to restore all people and all creation to right relation with God and each other through the life, death, and resurrection of Jesus Christ. Empowered by the Holy Spirit, the Church is called to participate in the restoration and reconciliation of all people to unity with God and each other in Christ. Thus the unity of the Church in service to God's promise of a restored and reconciled creation is fundamentally a missiological concern. Bishops who would participate in the 2008 Lambeth Conference would be invited to discover anew, and live more deeply into, their unity with God and each other in Christ as leaders called to serve and extend the *missio Dei*. Centring the Conference in the affirmation that the Church and its leadership, bishops in the case of Anglicanism, are fundamentally called to serve and advance God's mission in the world, the aim of the 2008 Lambeth Conference was primarily to equip bishops as leaders in mission and therein strengthen the Anglican Communion.

Missiological imperatives

The initial missiological imperative for the 2008 Lambeth Conference lay in another historical expression of the gathered Anglican Communion, namely Anglican Congresses. In the last century, there were three significant worldwide gatherings of Anglican lay people, deacons, priests, and bishops focusing on mission. These were known variously as Pan-Anglican, or Anglican, Congresses and were held in London in 1908, Minneapolis in 1954, and Toronto in 1963. These Congresses brought together thousands of Anglicans from every corner of the world to consider the missiological challenges and opportunities before Anglicans as a global family of churches. The Anglican Congress of 1963, in particular through its forward-looking vision of Anglican responsiveness to mission entitled 'Mutual Responsibility and Interdependence in Christ', helped to set the ecclesiological and missiological agenda for the contemporary Anglican Communion.

There have been a variety of efforts across Anglicanism in the last decade or so to hold another mission-focused Anglican Congress. The Anglican Consultative Council in its eleventh meeting in Dundee, Scotland in September 1999, in particular, called for an Anglican Congress to be held 'in association with the next Lambeth Conference'.[2] Because of changes in the office of the Archbishop of Canterbury, with Rowan Williams succeeding George Carey in 2003, planning for the combined Anglican Congress and Lambeth Conference was delayed. It was not until late 2003 that a Design Group for the combined Congress and Conference was named by Archbishop Williams and the first meeting of the Design Group did not occur until early 2004. The Group was specifically chosen to include Anglican leaders from a wide variety of contexts and backgrounds, all of whom had a primary commitment to mission. Included in the original Design Group were two lay women from Hong Kong and South Africa, a priest from the United States, bishops from Malawi, Cuba, Uruguay, South Africa, and Mauritius, and an archbishop from Melanesia. The Design Group was ably assisted by staff from the Anglican Communion office and Lambeth Palace (the office and residence of the Archbishop of Canterbury in London) and was later augmented by two additional bishops from England and Polynesia. The genuinely worldwide representation of these individuals (with a decidedly minority voice from the industrialized West) combined with a primary commitment to Christian mission in the many contexts and cultures that they represented was most significant to the planning process.

By mid-2004 planning for the combined Congress and Conference was well underway. The Design Group began to distinguish the two gatherings as having different missiological foci. In an attempt to keep the missiological 'horse before the cart' it was agreed that the more representative Congress would occur first and would focus on Anglican faithfulness to the mission of God in the world. The bishops' Conference would then follow and would concentrate on how Anglican leaders could best enable and empower Anglican churches in their faithfulness to the *missio Dei*. It was also decided that the site for the 2008 Anglican Congress and Lambeth Conference would be Cape Town, South Africa, reflecting the shift in Anglicanism to the 'Global South'.

Because of both logistical and financial limitations, it became clear in late 2004 that the Communion could not support an Anglican Congress in South Africa in 2008. This was highly disappointing for the Design Group, as well as local hosts in South Africa, not least the then Archbishop of Cape Town, Njongonkulu Ndungane, who had gone out of his way to make the Congress happen. Recognizing that the brief for the Design Group had significantly changed with the loss of the Congress, the Group offered to step down so that Archbishop Williams would have a free hand to put together a planning committee made up solely of bishops who would plan a bishops' only Lambeth Conference. Archbishop Williams would have none of it. Moved by the missiological focus of the combined Congress and Conference, and informed by his vocation as a theological educator, Archbishop Williams retained the original Design Group and charged them to do a new thing.

The new thing was to plan a Lambeth Conference whose primary agenda was to equip bishops as leaders in God's mission. He further believed that as bishops became more resourced as leaders in mission, the Anglican Communion itself would be drawn together in new ways of common service to the *missio Dei*. The missiological imperatives of the 2008 Lambeth Conference were clear: to equip bishops as leaders in God's mission and thus strengthen the common life and identity of the Anglican Communion. In his 2005 Advent Letter to Primates of the

Anglican Communion officially announcing plans for the 2008 Lambeth Conference Archbishop Williams emphasized this mission-driven focus for the Conference, saying: 'The main focus I long to see at this Conference is the better equipping of bishops to fulfil their task as agents and enablers of mission, as co-workers with God's mission in Jesus Christ.'[3] He reiterated the missiological imperatives in his welcome remarks in the *Official Programme and Event Guide* of the 2008 Lambeth Conference:

> The chief aims of our time together are, first, that we become more confident in our Anglican identity, by deepening our awareness of how we are responsible to and for each other; and second that we grow in energy and enthusiasm for our task of leading the work of mission in our church.[4]

Missiological process

With a free hand to design a new kind of Lambeth Conference oriented to equipping bishops as leaders in God's mission the Design Group, coming together in week-long meetings in London three times a year, set about imagining what kind of Conference would best serve the missiological imperative. Those bishops on the Design Group who had participated in the 1998 Lambeth Conference remembered with pain and sadness the contentious parliamentary debates of the last Conference, especially the debate over Resolution 1:10 on human sexuality.[5] With much prayerful discernment the Design Group concluded that following previous Lambeth Conference processes focusing on the drafting of theological reports supported by resolutions debated in parliamentary procedure would not best serve the Anglican Communion at this time. It was clear that a new, more relational and conversational process was needed if mutual understanding and common commitment to God's mission across the Anglican Communion was to be engendered among the bishops.[6]

This proposed relational and conversational process for Lambeth 2008 was embraced by the Archbishop of Canterbury and was in keeping with his perceived need for the Anglican Communion in the midst of difficult times. In October 2003 Archbishop Williams called an emergency meeting of the primates of the churches of the Anglican Communion to address the perceived crisis. Speaking to the BBC in October 2003 at the conclusion of the emergency meeting of primates to address the election and consent of Gene Robinson as Bishop of New Hampshire, an openly gay man living in a life-long partnered relationship with another man, the Archbishop of Canterbury said of the perceived crisis in the Anglican Communion: 'What complicates matters where the Anglican Church is concerned is that we're not a single monolithic body with a single decision-making authority. Our Communion depends a great deal on relationships rather than rules and it's those relationships that are strained at the moment . . .'[7]

The repair of such relationships and the desire to foster new relationships across differences in service to God's mission thus became central to the design of Lambeth 2008. Prior to the opening of the Conference in Canterbury, all bishops were given the opportunity to spend a week in various dioceses across the United Kingdom in order to witness and experience the lives of Anglicans in mission at the local level. This 'Hospitality Initiative' was hugely successful as it helped both the visiting bishops as well as lay people and clergy in England, Scotland and Wales to better understand their commonality as Anglicans in mission.

Arriving at the University of Kent in Canterbury, the venue for the 2008 Lambeth Conference, close to 700 Anglican bishops and ecumenical participants encountered a rich opportunity to come to know and resource each other as leaders in God's mission.[8] To do this the Conference utilized daily small Bible study groups (in the form of base Christian communities) made up of eight bishops from radically different contexts. While small group Bible study had been a part of at least the last few Lambeth Conferences, prioritizing the Bible study group as the key building block of the Conference process was new. An international team of biblical scholars and theologians from South Africa, England, Tanzania, the United States, India, Democratic Republic of Congo, and Aotearoa/New Zealand put together a sensitive and innovative contextual Bible study approach focusing on the 'I am . . . ' statements of Jesus in the Gospel of John. In over eighty groups of eight bishops each, those attending Lambeth 2008 encountered God and each other in a safe, face-to-face Christian community through the study of the Gospel of John and in the sharing of their own life stories and contexts.

The second significant new design element for the 2008 Lambeth Conference was larger *indaba* groups made up of five Bible study groups with a total of approximately forty bishops in each. *Indaba* is a Zulu word from South Africa originally connoting a meeting of chiefs or village leaders that 'gather for purposeful discussion' in community.[9] In sixteen separate *indaba* groups of forty bishops, where face-to-face accountabilities had already been established through the smaller Bible study groups, the bishops engaged common issues before the Anglican Communion.

Indabas met daily in the last half of the each morning following both Eucharist and the Bible study. Although resourced with suggested small group activities to discuss the assigned common daily topic or issue at hand, each *indaba* was free to design and follow its own life and group processes. The multi-vocal and multi-centric way of engaging tough questions before the Anglican Communion in the *indaba* groups, as compared to previously utilized parliamentary procedure, was underscored by Archbishop Williams in his 2008 Pentecost letter to the Bishops of the Anglican Communion in advance of the Lambeth Conference:

> I indicated in earlier letters that the shape of the Conference will be different from what many have been used to. We have listened carefully to those who have expressed their difficulties with Western and parliamentary styles of meeting, and the Design Group has tried to find a new style – a style more reflective of that Pentecost moment when all received the gift of speaking freely about Christ.
>
> At the heart of this will be the *Indaba* groups. *Indaba* is a Zulu word describing a meeting for purposeful discussion among equals. Its aim is not to negotiate a formula that will keep everyone happy but to go to the heart of an issue and

find what the true challenges are before seeking God's way forward. It is a method with parallels in many cultures, and it is close to what Benedictine monks and Quaker Meetings seek to achieve as they listen quietly together to God, in a community where all are committed to a fellowship of love and attention to each other and to the word of God.

Each day's work in this context will go forward with careful facilitation and preparation, to ensure that all voices are heard (and many languages also!). The hope is that over the two weeks we spend together, these groups will build a level of trust that will help us break down the walls we have so often built against each other in the Communion. And in combination with the intensive prayer and fellowship of the smaller Bible study groups, all this will result, by God's grace, in clearer vision and discernment of what needs to be done.[10]

Under-girding all of these opportunities for conversation and relationship building were an ordered worship and prayer life filled with vitality, joy, and celebration. Each day began with the bishops and their spouses gathering for Eucharist in a large tent especially designed as a worship space (affectionately known as the 'Big Top'). Leadership for each Eucharist was provided by bishops from different churches in the Anglican Communion and the tent was filled each morning with singing and visual images from around the world. Daily noon prayer was held in the context of each *indaba* group and then all of the bishops and spouses returned to the Big Top at the end of the day for Evening Prayer. In this ancient rhythm of an ordered daily prayer life, yet one that embraced various cultural expressions of worship from around the world, the bishops lived into their commonality in Christ while celebrating gifts from profoundly different cultural contexts.

Missiological content

The ten topics that the bishops considered sequentially in the *indabas* had a missiological trajectory initially focusing on the nature of God's mission in the wider world and moving to more inner-ecclesial matters of the Anglican Communion. To discern initial common ground the bishops began with the topic of Anglican identity. This built upon a preceding three-day retreat in the Cathedral at Canterbury led by the Archbishop of Canterbury on the theme 'God's Mission and a Bishop's Discipleship'. The bonding effect of beginning the whole conference with three days of prayer and study of the topic of the bishop in mission led by a renowned and gifted spiritual leader in one of the most sacred sites in Anglicanism cannot be overemphasized.

Days two and three of the *indabas* focused on the bishops' participation in God's mission through evangelism and social justice. These days gave a strong missiological grounding to the Walk for Witness in support of the Millennium Development Goals in London which followed on the first full Wednesday of the Conference. Starting at Whitehall and then proceeding alongside the Houses of Parliament and across the Lambeth Bridge ending at Lambeth Palace, more than 1300 bishops and spouses dressed in purple cassocks and national dress provided an inspiring witness to achieve the MDGs. In the courtyard of Lambeth Palace the marchers were stirred by the prophetic preaching of Prime Minister Gordon Brown, himself the son of a Church of Scotland minister, challenging the Church to be faithful to God's mission through advocacy for and direct action in the Millennium Development Goals.

Returning to Canterbury the bishops in their *indabas* then looked at how service to God's mission must be done cooperatively with sisters and brothers of other Christian traditions (ecumenism); as well as how the whole of creation needs to be safeguarded if the whole Church is to serve God in the wider world. The bishops then engaged the question of Christian witness in the midst of other faiths, recognizing that Christians are not the only people on the face of the earth.

Having considered mission in relationship to evangelism, social justice, ecumenism, the environment, and other faiths, the bishops then spent a day in a common programme with the parallel Spouses' Conference to consider how the use and abuse of power in the Church affects faithfulness to God's mission. The day with the spouses provided a transition as the bishops moved from the wider global context of God's mission into topics that are more specific to common life in the Anglican Communion. The bishops in *indaba* thus considered how the Bible forms and informs our service to God's mission and our common life together as Anglicans. The authority of the Bible and biblical interpretation led logically led to the question of how Anglicans understand human sexuality and the place of gay and lesbian people in the Church. The concluding few days of the *indaba* groups then focused on topics of Anglican common life with respect to the status of the *Windsor Report* and the proposed Anglican Covenant.[11]

The third major programmatic aspect of the 2008 Lambeth Conference was afternoon Self Select Sessions where bishops were free to choose among over one hundred different workshops, panels, lectures, and other hands-on learning opportunities. These Self Select Sessions were designed to equip bishops as leaders in God's mission through education and information sharing and were loosely organized around the topics/issues of the *indaba* groups. Mission agencies from around the Anglican Communion and the various official networks of the Communion were the primary resources for the Self Select Sessions, once again underscoring the missiological aim of the Conference.

As if worship, Bible study, *indabas* and Self Select Groups were not enough, in the evening the bishops had the opportunity to attend plenary gatherings to hear from major mission thinkers including Cardinal Ivan Dias, the Prefect for the Congregation for the Evangelization of Peoples at the Vatican, Brian McLaren, a leader in the 'emerging church movement', and Sir Jonathan Sacks, Chief Rabbi of the United Hebrew Congregations of the British Commonwealth. On the evenings when there were not official plenary presentations, space and hospitality were provided for any and all groups from across the Anglican Communion to host 'fringe events' as additional learning and social opportunities for the bishops. With this full complement of activities, the bishops were given incredibly rich and varied content as together they sought to be better equipped as leaders in God's mission.

Missiological implications

The missiological implications of the 2008 Lambeth Conference of Anglican bishops are hard to determine immediately and the full ramifications of the new direction of Lambeth might not be known for years to come. Still, one is able to offer a few tentative conclusions about the missiological vision of the most recent gathering of worldwide Anglican bishops.

It could be argued that on the surface the aim of Lambeth 2008 to equip bishops as leaders in God's mission and thus strengthen the Anglican Communion was pursued with diligence and faithfulness. At the Conference there was a concerted attempt to gather up the various conversations on the different topics addressed by the *indaba* groups through appointed 'listeners' in each of the sixteen groups. These 'listeners' worked tirelessly every night to draft representative reflections on each day's *indaba* conversations. These 'reflections' were then brought together in a multi-vocal document that was offered back to the bishops and the whole Anglican Communion under the title *Lambeth Indaba: Capturing Conversations and Reflections from the Lambeth Conference 2008 – Equipping Bishops for Mission and Strengthening Anglican Identity*.[12] As the title indicates, the document itself focuses on the imperative to equip bishops as leaders in God's mission and thus strengthen the Anglican Communion. In 'Lambeth *Indaba*' mission is clearly defined along the lines of the *missio Dei* as: 'the total action of God in Christ by the power of the Holy Spirit – creating, redeeming, sanctifying – for the sake of the whole world' (§19). The priority given to God's mission, thus defined, is clear in the document as 80 of the 161 paragraphs are dedicated to the bishop in mission, with 63 other paragraphs focusing on strengthening Anglican identity, and the remain 18 paragraphs being introductory in nature. This emphasis on mission, and more particularly the role of bishops in God's mission, is not to be taken lightly. It underscores the reality that the bishops who attended Lambeth were genuinely equipped in new ways to serve God's mission in the world.

Not everyone, however, including both bishops who were at Lambeth 2008 and those who were not, was pleased with either the 'reflections document' or the new direction of the Lambeth Conference. Those who were looking to Lambeth to be the arbitrator of all things Anglican or a final decision point on such matters as the proposed Anglican Covenant were not pleased with its new design. Some even accused the Archbishop of Canterbury of eschewing parliamentary process in order to avoid tough decisions. In conspiratorial terms some even accused the archbishop of wanting to disempower so-called 'Global South' Anglican bishops who would have been a majority in a parliamentary plenary at Lambeth if all had attended and if they all voted in a block. But Archbishop Williams defended the missiological vision of the Lambeth Conference and its relational, conversational and prayerful approach, saying:

> Some reactions to my original invitation have implied that meeting for prayer, mutual spiritual enrichment and development of ministry is somehow a way of avoiding difficult issues. On the contrary: I would insist that *only* in such a context can we usefully address divisive issues. If our difficulties have their root in whether or how far we can recognize the same gospel and ministry in diverse places and policies, we need to engage more not less directly with each other. This is why I have repeatedly said that an invitation to Lambeth does not constitute a certificate of orthodoxy but simply a challenge to pray seriously together and to seek a resolution that will be as widely owned as may be.
>
> And this is also why I have said that the refusal to meet can be a refusal of the cross – and so of the resurrection. We are being asked to see our handling of conflict and potential division as part of our maturing both as pastors and as disciples.[13]

And it is true that some did refuse to meet by not attending the Lambeth Conference of 2008. Conspicuously absent were over one hundred bishops from the Anglican Churches of Nigeria, Uganda, Rwanda and Sydney, Australia. Ironically, the more that Lambeth 2008 engendered a greater sense of commonality in God's mission among the bishops who attended, the greater the gulf that could develop between those Anglican bishops that came to Canterbury and those that did not.

An unscientific sampling of initial responses to the Lambeth Conference 2008 shows that it was hugely successful in its conversational and relational approach to equipping bishops as leaders in God's mission and thus strengthening the Anglican Communion. At Lambeth itself many bishops expressed a desire to somehow meet in their *indaba* groups in the future, and calls were heard for more frequent Lambeth Conferences. *Indaba*s are appearing in various diocesan and provincial gatherings around the Anglican Communion and both the Anglican Consultative Council and the Primates' Meeting are considering how to utilize *indabas* in their next gatherings. And significant appreciation has been shown in all corners of the Anglican Communion for Archbishop Williams' vision and leadership in doing a new thing with Lambeth. The transformative experience of Lambeth 2008 is summed up in a letter from a bishop in the Church of North India to the Revd Canon Phil Groves, Facilitator of the 'Listening Process' around issues of human sexuality in the Anglican Communion.

I am serving the people of the Diocese of Amritsar, Church of North India, in the states of Punjab, Himachal Pradesh and Jammu & Kashmir. I came to attend the Lambeth Conference with a lot of questions in my mind about the issue of human sexuality as I knew this issue has threatened the unity in the Anglican Communion. Coming from a conservative back-ground I was not even prepared to listen to any person who supported the gay and lesbian people. However, the *Indaba* experience has changed my opinion. After listening to the stories of bishops coming from different cultural contexts I have become aware of the pain and agony people have to bear because of our attitude towards each other. Further, I am

convinced that despite their different and often opposite positions all are committed to live and grow within the Anglican
family. The binding force in a family is love. If we love one another we learn to transcend our differences and don't hesitate
to sacrifice our own interests for the sake of the family unity.
This is possible only when we are willing to listen to each
other. The amount of sacrifices I make is dependent on the
depth of my love and intimacy of my relationship.

As for me I have decided not to be hasty in judging the
gay and the lesbians. I wish to learn more about their life and
problems. I have also decided to regularly pray for them. I
wish to encourage the other members of the Anglican Communion to do the same.[14]

No one in the Anglican Communion believes that the difficulties and challenges before the Communion have suddenly disappeared because bishops from vastly different cultures can now
better see and understand both the commonalities they share
and the distinctive contextual particularities they inhabit. But of
the close to seven hundred bishops who did attend the Lambeth
Conference of 2008, most would agree that they are recommit-
ted to God and each other in Christ and are better equipped to
serve God's mission in the world. And therein is hope for the
Anglican Communion and its faithfulness to the *missio Dei*.

Bibliography

Chadwick, Owen, 'Introduction' in Roger Coleman (ed.), *Resolutions
of the Twelve Lambeth Conferences 1867–1988*, Toronto: Anglican
Book Centre, 1992

Douglas, Ian T., 'Anglicans Gathering for God's Mission: A Missiological Ecclesiology for the Anglican Communion', *Journal of Anglican
Studies* 2.2, December 2004, pp. 9–40

Rosenthal, James and Rodgers, Margaret (eds.), *The Communion We
Share: Anglican Consultative Council XI, Scotland*, Harrisburg, PA:
Morehouse Publishing, 2000

Ward, Kevin, *A History of Global Anglicanism*, Cambridge: Cambridge
University Press, 2006

Notes

1 First published in the *International Bulletin of Missionary Research* 33 (2009), pp. 3–6.

2 The rationale as to why the Anglican Congress should be held in association with the Lambeth Conference is beyond the scope of this paper, although it is an important study as to power struggles in emerging Anglican ecclesiology. See 'Resolution 14: Anglican Congress' (Rosenthal and Rodgers: 2000, pp. 349–50).

3 A primate is the head bishop, archbishop, metropolitan, or presiding bishop, in each of the 38 churches of the Anglican Communion. See: '2005 Advent Letter by the Archbishop of Canterbury', http://www.archbishopofcanterbury.org/870?q=2005+Advent+Letter

4 *Official Programme & Event Guide*, London: The Lambeth Conference, 2008, p. 2.

5 See: *The Official Report of the Lambeth Conference of 1998*, Harrisburg, PA: Morehouse Publishing for the Anglican Communion, 1999, pp. 381–2.

6 For a fuller discussion of the missiological significance of relationships across difference in the Anglican Communion see Douglas: 2004.

7 'Radio Interview with the Archbishop of Canterbury', Anglican Communion News Service #3640, 18 October 2003, http://anglicancommunion.org/acns/articles/36/25/acns3640.html

8 The fact that ecumenical participants were considered 'full participants' in the Conference and not guests or observers was continually emphasized as a sign of a shared common calling in God's mission.

9 Reflections on the 'Essence of *Indaba*' offered by The Most Revd Thabo Makgoba, Archbishop of Cape Town and member of the Lambeth Conference Design Group, in *Worship and Indaba Group Resources*, London: Lambeth Conference, 2008, section on *indaba* groups, pp. 1–2.

10 'Archbishop of Canterbury's Pentecost Letter to the Bishops of the Anglican Communion', Anglican Communion News Service #4403, 13 May 2008, http://www.anglicancommunion.org/acns/news.cfm/2008/5/13/acns4403

11 *The Windsor Report*, drafted by the Lambeth Commission on Communion and released in late 2004, is a significant study of the current and emerging ecclesiology of the Anglican Communion. Its recommendations, including a proposed 'Anglican Covenant', are under consideration across the churches of the Anglican Communion in what is generally considered 'The Windsor Process'.

12 "Lambeth *Indaba*: Capturing Conversations and Reflections from the Lambeth Conference 2008 – Equipping Bishops for Mission and Strengthening Anglican Identity." at: http://www.lambethconference.org/reflections/document.cfm

13 'Archbishop of Canterbury's Advent Letter', Anglican Communion News Service #4354, 14 December 2007, http://www.anglican-communion.org/acns/news.cfm/2007/12/14/acns4354

14 Private letter from Revd Canon Phil Groves to authors who contributed to the book *The Anglican Communion and Homosexuality*, 13 October 2008. Quoted with permission.

13

AFTER LAMBETH—WHERE NEXT?

An Afterword

Martyn Percy

An apocryphal tale from the vast annals of Anglican folklore tells of an occasion when someone wrote to the Archbishop of Canterbury to thank him for something he had said on the radio. It was an appreciative letter, and the correspondent kindly enclosed a cheque for £10 – made payable to 'the Church of England'. It caused some amusement at Lambeth Palace, for strange though this may seem, it could not be cashed. There is no organization or bank account bearing that name. True, there is the Church of England Pensions Board, various divisions concerned with ministry and education, several dozen dioceses, and of course the Church Commissioners – all of which refer to the Church of England. But no bank account bears the sole nomenclature. The cheque had to be returned with a note: 'Thank you – but do you think you could be more specific?'

The problem is not as odd as it seems. It would be rather like me receiving a cheque for £10 made out to 'the Percy family'. Whilst grateful, I would be unable to cash it. To which branch of the family does the cheque refer? Aunts, uncles and cousins may claim an interest. To say nothing of the handful of readers of this concluding piece who might share my surname, and are already experiencing a frisson of excitement at the prospect of an unexpected windfall.

It is perhaps no accident that when Jesus turned his metaphorically disposed mind to the subject of the Church, he reached for a rather riveting analogy: 'I am the vine, you are the branches' (John 15.5). It is a suggestive, economical phrase, where one suspects that the use of the plural is quite deliberate. Even for an apparently homogenous organization like the Church of England (let alone the Anglican Communion), 'branches' offers a better descriptive fit than most of the labels on offer. It suggests inter-dependence yet difference; unity and diversity; commonality yet independence; continuity and change; pruning, yet fruitfulness.

In other words, the analogy sets up a correlation between particularity and catholicity. This is, of course, a struggle that Anglicans are all too familiar with. There is a constant wrestling for the 'true' identity of Anglicanism; a struggle to reach a point where its soul ceases to be restless, and becomes more fully self-conscious. But in the meantime, the Church finds itself easy prey to a variety of interest-led groups (from the theological left and right) that continually assert their freedoms over any uneasy consensus. The assumption made here is that any one branch is 'free' from the others.

Technically, this is correct. But the illusion of independence threatens to impoverish a profound catholic aspect of Anglicanism. The right to express and practise particularity is too often preferred to the self-imposed restraint that is hinted at by a deeper catholicity. Thus, one branch will exercise its assumed privilege of freedom – whether that is fiscal, political, theological or moral – over the others. The consequence of this is all too obvious. The branches attempt to define the vine.

Which is why issues of gender, sexuality and polity quickly become the primary foci that distinguish one branch from another, rather than secondary indicators of emphasis that are subjugated to an innate connectedness to the true vine. There seems to be little understanding that an unfettered claim to act freely can actually become anti-social, or even unethical. Great freedom comes with great responsibility.

Interestingly, bishops have a vital role here in presiding over diversity whilst maintaining unity. This is why the key to some of the current divisive Anglican dilemmas may lie in dioceses and provinces becoming more consciously expressive of their catholic identity, and celebrating their coherence amidst their diversity. A diocese is more than an arbitrary piece of territory. It is a part of a larger, living, organic whole. It is a branch of the vine. Therefore, exercising its freedom and expressing its particularity is less important than maintaining its connectedness. The trouble starts when any specific branch purports to speak and act for the whole, but without sufficient humility. Naturally, such restraint need not impose limits on diversity. It merely asks that the consequences of exercising one's freedom be more fully weighed.

As Anglican primates continue to meet after the Lambeth Conference, there will be much to carry forward in contemplation and conversation. How to hold together in the midst of tense, even bitter diversity. How to be one, yet many. How to be faithfully catholic, yet authentically local. In all of this, an ethic of shared restraint – borne out of a deep catholicity – may have much to offer the Anglican Communion. Without this, Anglicans risk being painfully lost in the issues that beset the Church – unable to see the wood for the trees. Or perhaps, as Jesus might have said, unable to see the vine for the branches.

It is partly for this reason that I continue to remain uneasy about the potential *use* of something like the proposed Anglican Covenant (as an arguably useful template for unity) rather than the actuality of the drafted text. Documents of this kind invariably contain the (potentially problematic) capacity to occlude their movement from textuality to instrumentality. And instruments, to be useful, require functions and authoritatively licensed users. So in one sense, I am not clear what the Covenant adds to the current instruments of unity within the worldwide Communion. One can see that it signals an intensification of the need to be in broad agreement on certain issues; to act with restraint, with provinces thinking more about the 'catholic' implications of their preferred local practice; and to strengthen the role of the primates in the expression and delimitation of a common mind and shared practices.

Correspondingly, the question necessarily arises: who, or what bodies, will use the Covenant, and against what or whom, and how? Most of the dis-ease about the Covenant, one suspects, lies here – and not with the text itself. I think that the Communion will need to be reassured that the Covenant is not a specifically targeted text that is directed against apparent pain or problems (i.e., is neither palliative nor punitive), but is rather a document that arises naturally and organically out of our common life, and expresses our desire to clarify and deepen our bonds of affection. Put more sharply, it will serve the Communion better if it can be seen to express the shared wisdom that we seek, as well as being a celebration of our unity, diversity and collective witness to Jesus Christ and the gospel, rather than a text that is imposed unilaterally.

Closely linked to this observation, one might say that our Anglican ecclesiology is to be seen not only in terms of shared and agreed propositions, but also as a shared set of acquired skills and practices. We are formed not only by what we say, but by the manner and modes of our expression. In this regard, the censure of Bishop James Pike (over forty years ago, in 1966) merits repetition:

> When Episcopalians are questioned about the supposed orthodoxy or heterodoxy of one of their number, their most likely response is to ask whether or not [this person] wishes – sincerely and responsibly – to join them in a celebration of God's being and goodness in the prayers and worship of the Prayer Book. Assuming [this person's] integrity, they would not be likely to press the question beyond that point. (Bayne: 1976, p. 21)

All of us in the Communion, I am sure, would accept the precedence and priority that can be placed upon urgent matters in relation to identity and decisiveness. However, our 'common' life and prayer together is also an expression of our commitment to patience; and an understanding that the relationship between practice and belief is a complex one within the Communion. As Stephen Sykes (amongst others) has pointed out, it is inconceivable that there has ever been complete agreement on the identity of Christianity. Part of the genius of our faith lies in its contestability. Moreover, conflicts can only really be made explicit and *managed* through processes of theological reflection – but, I should add, not necessarily resolved.

So I would want to ask at this point: is it envisaged that something like the Covenant helps us to manage and reflect upon our difficulties, or to resolve them? The former produces clarity and charity, but not necessarily at the expense of diversity. The latter, it seems to me, could be a rather ambitious enterprise for any denomination to contemplate – but equally not impossible. Clearly, doctrinal discussions do reach a point of *consensus* when they become decisions.

However, and without in any way wishing to undervalue consensus, I would also add that there is something to be said for the Anglican virtue of un-decidability. 'Un-decidability' is 'procrastination with purpose': the exercise of extreme patience that enables polities to wrestle with high levels of seemingly unresolvable tension. Make a decision too early – even the right one – and you may win the argument (note: may); but you will probably lose the people. In other words, means may matter more than ends. This principle – indeed, virtue – is something that the Covenant document or such like often fails to acknowledge. The practice of patience over and against precision is what is at stake here; recognizing that a leap to the latter will leave many stranded and languishing in the former.

This takes me back, neatly enough, to the questions around the use of the Covenant, rather than being concerned with the text itself. Indeed, I think a debate on the minutiae of the text, although clearly important, is only one half of the equation that needs to be considered. The fundamental question remains: how do we go about making decisions in relation to practice in such a way as to maintain the continuity of Christianity? Our 'problem', apparently, is that our identity partly resides in the celebration of breadth, and in a diversity of practice. And occasionally in a lack of clarity about how some local practices might impinge upon our collective catholic identity. I remain convinced, here, that we need to continue to carefully distinguish between essential practices (say in regard to doctrine, unity, etc.) and contextualized practices that are essentially secondary issues.

It seems to me that the promise and anticipation of the Covenant, in many ways, have already achieved some clarity in regard to the issues it seeks to address. There is more evidence – across the Communion – of patience, restraint and the practice of shared wisdom in the wake of the issues and circumstances that have prompted the Covenant document. This suggests that the very possibility of the Covenant (rather than its actuality) may have already achieved much. Whilst a few perceive the document as a threat, and a few perceive it to be inadequate, the majority have already come to see that its gradual formulation is an opportunity to rediscover consensus in the midst of diversity, and rediscover the discipline (and therefore some limits) of what is entailed in journeying together within the Anglican tradition.

However, this same observation also prompts me to urge the primates (and other instruments of unity) towards the continued practice of patience, and to plea for pausing, reflection and space before committing ourselves to any kind of premature foreclosure. If the mere *possibility* of the Covenant has already helped us move to a place of deeper collective self-discipline and critical self-reflection, then there is a powerful argument for *prolonging* this period, where a greater degree of wisdom and charity has already been found, even amidst some considerable tensions. I am reminded of Wittgenstein's metaphor of the rope, where he draws our attention to how its strength depends on the tiny individual fibres that overlap and interlace. Our Communion – a rich tapestry of threads and colours – is, I believe, rediscovering its strength and identity through these testing times. So I would hope that the Covenant document, when it eventually and ultimately comes into being, would be able to find a more reassuring and celebratory rhetorical cadence than it has at present – one that focused less on the fear of unravelling, and more on the deeper reality of our becoming.

This is a more urgent task than it might at first appear, because the discernment that is called for here is not simply one that picks its way through interpretative differences and then makes decisions. Such a strategy merely divides and conquers. The task is how to live with difference, rather than avoiding this. Our call is to a 'commonality' with diversity; unity with differences. And we affirm and witness to breadth because we sense that God is more than the sum of our parts; even though this makes for some difficult conversations amongst ourselves.

It is clearly no secret that the worldwide Anglican Communion contains tensions on how to read Scripture. Everyone knows that Anglicans can agree on what the Bible says: but are on shakier ground when it comes to a common mind on meaning. On the surface, the manifest difficulties appear to be centred on issues such as sexuality, gender, the right use of the Bible, and the appropriate interpretation of Scripture. It is therefore possible to narrate the schismatic tendencies in Anglicanism with reference to authority, theology and ecclesial power. But on its own, as a thesis, this is clearly inadequate, as such tensions have existed within Anglicanism from the outset. There has not been a single century in which Anglicanism has not wrestled with its identity; it is by nature a polity that draws on a variety of competing theological traditions. Its very appeal lies in its own distinctive hybridity.

Another way of reading the current difficulties is to register that the polity itself is expressive of competing but covert cultural convictions. One might say, for example, that current Anglican difficulties began with the American Revolution (or War of Independence), which caused American Anglicans to re-conceive their faith as Republicans rather than Royalists. The emergence of Samuel Seabury as the first American Anglican bishop (consecrated, incidentally, by Scottish bishops rather than by the Archbishop of Canterbury) marks a seminal moment in the identity of Anglicanism. Although the gesture itself, at least on the surface, is not significant, it comes to represent the emergence of two competing streams of ecclesial polity within a single Communion.

The first is Royalist, bound to a culture that is aligned with hierarchy and obedience that is at least linked to divine right and ordering. But the second, which is Republican, is essentially democratic in orientation, and therefore about the rights of the people more than the princes and prelates. Moreover, there is a modification to the Royalist paradigm that needs to be factored in, for it is not an ancient quasi-feudal system, but rather that which emerged out of the seventeenth-century English Civil War, which had deposed outright notions of kingship, but had then restored kingly power, albeit checked by new forms of democratic and parliamentary power.

There is some sense in which a range of current Anglican difficulties can be read against these deep underground cultural streams that eventually cause the apparent seismic doctrinal shifts. The election of Gene Robinson (a genial, gay clergyman) as Bishop of New Hampshire is an expression of North American faith in the gift of democracy (from God) and the inalienable right to choose. A people who were chosen – liberated, as it were, from the yoke of colonial patrimony – are now called upon by God to continue exercising their God-given rights to choose. Thus, the will of a foreign power – or even the mild intervention of a friendly Archbishop of Canterbury – will be seen as an act of hostility and despotic feudalism.

These two streams of power, deeply embedded in their respective cultures (not unlike Churchill's notion of two nations divided by a common language) is all it takes to produce two kinds of very different theological grammar within the same Communion. And when such differences are mapped on to the worldwide Anglican Communion, and emerging post-colonial identity is taken account of within developing nations, which are suspicious of both the old ordering of kingly power and the apparent 'consumerism' of the democratic stream, the stage is set for some major divisions to emerge, which will disguise themselves in doctrinal and ecclesial difference.

Yeats' poem mourned that 'things fall apart; the centre cannot hold'. But the centre was always contested, not settled. So what is to be done? No one solution presents itself. Recognizing that there are cultural factors in shaping and individuating churches is important. Valuing diversity alongside unity will be vital. And praying fervently with Jesus 'that we may all be one' will also be crucial – although we might perhaps mutter in the same breath: 'but thank God we are all different'.

Of course, much ink was spilled in the run-up to the Lambeth Conference, playing up these differences, as though they were manifestly signs of weakness and hopelessness. This accounts for the media-fest writing off Anglicanism, attacking the leadership of the Archbishop of Canterbury, and pointing to the gathering forces of conservatism in movements such as Gafcon (Global Anglican Futures Conference) and FOCA (Fellowship of Confessing Anglicans). The media reporting prior to the Conference was mostly gloomy and doom-laden: about as helpful as a phalanx of Job's comforters staffing the telephones at a local branch of the Samaritans. Yet Anglicans hardly need the media to provide the dubious comforts of depressive consolation, for they are very good at squabbling amongst themselves. Mired in a culture of blaming and mutual castigation, Anglicans all but seem to have lost the knack of cultivating and practising the virtues of tolerance and patience amidst their differences and diversity.

The roots of this particular Anglican difficulty do not need spelling out. The election of Gene Robinson to the See of New Hampshire was, despite whatever personal merits he may have had, regarded by others as an example of North American individualism cloaked in the rhetoric of progression and justice. The trouble with such a decision is the lack of regard for a wider catholicity, and the attendant responsibility this carries. Furthermore, the Episcopal electors of New Hampshire should perhaps have paused to reflect that the (oft overlooked) cousins of individualism are impatience and intolerance.

So from the minute that Gene Robinson was consecrated, the unholy and viral trinity of individualism, impatience and intolerance was unleashed, and has rapidly spread to very different quarters of the Anglican Communion, yet with unsurprisingly similar results. So that now, each part of the worldwide Church, whether liberal or conservative, white or black, can claim to be true and right, whilst expressing their individuality, irritation and annoyance with all those they disagree with.

But the only antidote to this plague of rashness remains a tried and tested Anglican remedy: the recovery and infusion of those qualities that are embedded in the Gospels, and in deeper and denser forms of ecclesial polity. Namely ones that are formed out of patience, forbearance, catholicity, moderation – and a genuine love for the reticulate blend of diversity and unity that forms so much of the richness for Anglican life. But in the woof and weave of the Church, these virtues have been lost – or rather mislaid – in a miscibility of debates that are marked by increasing levels of tension and stress.

Yet if this sounds like too much of a tangle for some, it is interesting to note that when Jesus reaches for metaphors that describe the kingdom of God (and, by implication, the possibility and potential of churches), he often uses untidy images. 'I am the vine, you are the branches' comes to mind. No stately cedar tree of Lebanon here; or even an English oak or Californian redwood. Jesus chooses a sprawling, knotted plant that requires patience and careful husbandry.

In another short parable, Jesus compares the kingdom of heaven to a mustard seed – one of the smallest seeds that grows into 'the greatest of all shrubs and sprouts large branches' (Mark 4.30–32). The image is ironic, and possibly even satirical. One has every right to expect the kingdom of God to be compared to the tallest and strongest of trees. But Jesus likens the Church to something that sprouts up quite quickly from almost nothing, and then develops into an ungainly sprawling shrub that cannot even hold up a bird's nest. (But the birds, note, have the wit to find shelter under the branches.)

The Anglican Communion, then, can take some comfort from the lips of Jesus. Like the mustard seed, it can be an untidy sprawling shrub. Like a vine, it can be knotted and gnarled. Neither plant is much to look at. But Jesus knew what he was doing when he compared his kingdom to these two plants. He was saying something quite profound about the nature of the Church: it will be rambling, extensive and just a tad jumbled. And that's the point. Jesus seems to understand that it often isn't easy to find your place in neat and tidy systems. Or maybe you'll feel alienated and displaced. But in a messy and slightly disorderly church, and in an unordered and rather rumpled institution, all may find a home.

So there are no easy answers of the post-Lambeth question 'Where next?'. Anglicanism is primarily a patient form of polity, because it gives time to issues, questions and dilemmas. And time and patience are rooted in charity and forebearance. We let the wheat grow with the tares; we do not separate the sheep from the goats. It will take more than one Lambeth Conference to work through the differences that currently appear to divide kith from kin, and to work out what they all mean. But in the meantime, all Anglicans need to heed one of the many calls from the Book of Common Prayer. In the 1549 Prayer Book this call was placed immediately before the reception of Holy Communion; indeed, it is the last call before there can be any kind of Holy Communion:

> Ye that do truly and earnestly repent you of your sins, and are in love and charity with your neighbours, and intend to lead a new life, following the commandments of God, and walking from henceforth in his holy ways: Draw near with faith . . .

Bibliography

Bayne, S., *Theological Freedom and Social Responsibility*, New York, Seabury, 1976

STUDY GUIDE

Stephen Pickard – The Bishop and Anglican Identity

1) In what ways have you experienced Anglican people supporting and sharing the bishop's role in reconnecting people 'to each other, to the earth, and to God'?
2) How might connections between people, the earth and God be deepened in your local context? Who is responsible for this?

Clive Handford – Celebrating Common Ground

1) How would it change the character of the Anglican Communion were the Archbishop of Canterbury to start behaving like a 'headmaster'?
2) 'A house divided' . . . united by 'bonds of affection' . . . What words would you choose to describe the Anglican Communion?

James Tengatenga – Proclaiming the Good News

1) In what ways does the Church 'speak the language of the times' as it seeks to communicate Good News?
2) 'The bishop is only one person and the demands on his time are such that he cannot do it all.' What, then, is your own role in communicating the Good News?

Johannes T. Seoka – Transforming Society

1) How would you like to see the Church shaping society, so that people come to enjoy 'a sacred space that affirms human dignity'?

2) 'The Church as a whole must never allow itself to be tied to any political party.' What do you regard as legitimate ways for the Church to work towards social justice?

Geoffrey Rowell – The Bishop, Other Churches, and God's Mission 1

1) 'Anglican identity cannot be divorced from the challenges posed to us by the sheer hindrance caused by the disunity of Christians.' Under what circumstances, if any, might Anglican disunity be regarded as anything other than a hindrance?
2) What should happen when, in good conscience, the quest for justice comes into conflict with the quest for unity?

John William Hind – The Bishop, Other Churches, and God's Mission 2

1) What problems arise when the Church 'in the world' instead becomes 'of the world'?
2) What does it mean to belong to a church that 'may often get it wrong'?

Christopher Epting – The Bishop, Other Churches, and God's Mission 3

1) To what extent can a bishop be described as a 'symbol of unity' in an openly divided church?
2) What ways might we find to work more closely with Christians from other churches?

Suheil S. Dawani – Engaging with a Multi-Faith World 1

1) How effective a tool is a 'ministry of presence' when engaging with people of other faiths?

2) What significance do you attach to Christian engagement with people of other faiths in the Holy Land?

Michael Jackson – Engaging with a Multi-Faith World 2

1) Presence and engagement . . . embassy and hospitality . . . sending and abiding . . . How useful are these words in engaging with human difference in your home context?
2) If 'the spaces in which we meet one another do not belong to either host or guest; they belong to God', what should we look for in the encounter?

Saw John Wilme – Engaging with a Multi-Faith World 3

1) What lessons from the successes and limitations of inter-faith encounter in Myanmar can usefully be applied to your home context?
2) If you were charged with the task of educating people about inter-faith engagement, which single insight would you want to pass on?

N. Thomas Wright – The Bishop and Living Under Scripture

1) What does it mean to be a 'Scripture-shaped praying people'?
2) 'An unfinished play, in which those who belong to Jesus Christ are now called to be actors, taking forward the drama to its intended conclusion.' How does this fit with your understanding of Scripture?

Ian T. Douglas – Equipping for God's Mission

1) What are the strengths and weaknesses of a church where leadership emerges out of a 'relational and conversational' process?

2) Can you imagine any purpose for an *indaba* conversation in your parish?

Group activity

Several bishops spoke of the importance of praying together in the retreat at the beginning of the Lambeth Conference, and of the value of listening to one another through the *indaba* groups. The following provides a structure for groups to engage meditatively with some of the questions raised by the bishops.

Before you begin the exercise, choose a Bible passage and a question from the list above.

1) Light a candle to indicate the beginning of a short time of silence.

2) The silence is followed by one person slowly reading a short passage of Scripture twice, followed by silence of a few minutes.

Possible readings:

Psalm 131

Isaiah 65.8–9

Matthew 17.1–5

James 3.17–18

3) When everyone is ready, go slowly round the group, so that everyone has the chance to say how those words speak to them.

4) When everyone has spoken, one person then reads the question aloud.

5) Go round the group allowing each person to respond to the question. Then go round the group again, allowing each person to respond to something that has already been said.

6) Silence is kept again to enable people to reflect prayerfully upon what has been said, until the candle is blown out.

7) Informal conversation can follow.

NAME INDEX